WHAT PEOPLE ARE SAYIN

SO YOU WANT T
A FREELANCE WK⌐⌐⌐

A knowledgeable writer on spiritual subjects, her easy-to-read style makesthe topic very accessible.
Sue Ricketts, Editor - take a break's fate & Fortune

Deborah consistently comes up with ideas that our readers will love – and follows up with great features that are entertaining, informative and tailored to our market.
Karan Byrom, Editor - *My Weekly*

I am impressed by Deborah's diligence to her profession and the care taken to ensure all articles submitted are engaging, relevant to our readership and, most importantly, well written. She has an understanding for delivering appropriate copy that requires no editing and pitching features that will make a difference to our readers' lives.
Aine Toner, Editor *Woman's Way Ireland*

Deborah is an outstanding journalist with indepth knowledge of the market. Her writing is fluent, entertaining, accessible and informative – and is always of such a high standard, it requires little, if any editing. She gets what our readers want and delivers every time.
Mary Bryce, Editor, *Chat Its fate*

Deborah has worked as a freelance writer for *Natural Health* for three years and provides in-depth and well researched features that appeal to our readers. She is an asset to the team.
Emma Van Hinsbergh, Editor, *Natural Health Magazine*

LAWRENCEBURG PUBLIC LIBRARY DISTRICT

LAWRENCEBURG PUBLIC LIBRARY

So You Want to Be a Freelance Writer

Writing for magazines, newspapers and beyond

So You Want to Be a Freelance Writer

Writing for magazines, newspapers and beyond

Deborah Durbin

**COMPASS
BOOKS**

Winchester, UK
Washington, USA

First published by Compass Books, 2013
Compass Books is an imprint of John Hunt Publishing Ltd., Laurel House, Station Approach,
Alresford, Hants, SO24 9JH, UK
office1@jhpbooks.net
www.johnhuntpublishing.com
www.compass-books.net

For distributor details and how to order please visit the 'Ordering' section on our website.

Text copyright: Deborah Durbin 2011

ISBN: 978 1 78099 492 5

All rights reserved. Except for brief quotations in critical articles or reviews, no part of this
book may be reproduced in any manner without prior written permission from the publishers.

The rights of Deborah Durbin as author have been asserted in accordance with the Copyright,
Designs and Patents Act 1988.

A CIP catalogue record for this book is available from the British Library.

Design: Stuart Davies

Printed in the USA by Edwards Brothers Malloy

808.02 DUR
Durbin, Deborah
So you want to be a
    freelance writer? :
    writing for magazines,
    newspapers and beyond

35340635307910   Mar 13

We operate a distinctive and ethical publishing philosophy in all
areas of our business, from our global network of authors to
production and worldwide distribution.

CONTENTS

Introduction

I have worked as a freelance writer and journalist for the past 15 years and in that time I have written for most of the UK national women's magazines and many national newspapers. I have had 11 books published, have ghost-written three other books, been a columnist for two national magazines, taught writing classes and have been a local newspaper editor. I have written for publications in the UK, Ireland and America and all this in the name of being a freelance writer.

During my career as a freelance writer I have written for everything from tabloids to the broadsheets and everything in between, and have learned a lot of tips and tricks of the trade. By compiling this book I will hopefully make things a little easier for you to break in to the competitive world of freelance writing. I hope you enjoy the book.

The Advantages and Disadvantages of Freelance Writing

Working as a freelance writer is one of the best jobs I've ever had – and I've had a fair few; from temping in offices to stuffing teddy bears to be sold in Harrods! But as with anything in life, it's not fun and games all of the time. Sometimes it's lonely, particularly if you are a naturally sociable person and are used to bouncing ideas off other people. And then there are the rejections that you have to accept come as part of the job and the occasional annoyance that an editor has liked your idea so much that he/she has chosen to give it to a staff-writer to write instead of commission you (yes, this really does happen; not often, but sometimes). Below is a list of the pros and cons of becoming a freelance writer, just so you know what you're letting yourself in for.

Advantages

You get to work when you want

This is the best bit of the job for me because I have a family that takes priority in my life, so any job that can work around that is a godsend, if you ask me. The majority of freelance writers work from the comfort of their own home (which is both a blessing and a curse at times – see the disadvantages section) and this means that you can usually juggle work around family commitments, even if it means writing up an article when the children are fed, bathed and in bed. So long as you submit your copy on time, no one is any the wiser that you were writing it up in the middle of the night, in your pyjamas.

The money is good

Obviously, when you start out as a freelance writer you cannot demand the same fee as an established professional (see why writing for free is good) but once you have established yourself as a good and efficient writer, you will be in demand. Many publications now prefer to call on a bank of good freelance writers rather than take on additional staff-writers, to whom they have to pay a salary.

You get to learn something new every day

To succeed in this industry a good freelancer needs to be adaptable to whatever he/she writes about. If you only write about the same subject, your potential for work will dry up pretty quickly. If you can learn to write to order, not only do you learn about different subjects, but you also multiply your chances of getting work. In addition, it's a great feeling when you research a subject you had no prior knowledge about and end up with a commission for it. I have written about so many subjects I initially knew nothing about, from cellular memory to Chinese face-reading and I never tire of it – not to mention you'll always have something to talk about at a party!

You meet some very interesting people

One great aspect of being a freelance writer is that you get to meet some fabulous characters through interviews and very often they become lifelong friends. I once helped an elderly gentleman to get his memoirs down on paper and 10 years on, we are still in touch with each other. Again, I interviewed a lady who has saved the lives of 15 other people in her lifetime after taking a first-aid course and we are still in touch today. Everyone knows something that another person doesn't and it amazes me how many lovely people have come into my life on the basis of a story I've been writing.

Anything related to your work is a tax expense

So your notebooks, laptop, PC, pens, any stamps you buy, a

percentage of your utility bills, printers and cartridges, phone calls for interview purposes, among other things are all expenses and you will be surprised at how many things you buy on a weekly basis that count as such. You should always keep a record (and receipts if possible) of everything you purchase for the purpose of writing.

No two days are the same

As a freelancer no two days are the same: one day you might be writing a press-release for a book, the next you might be interviewing a celebrity, or reporting on a court case or researching pension plans for a commissioned article or writing a novel, or interviewing someone about their ghostly encounters. The diversity of freelance writing means that you lead a very interesting life and in turn you don't get bored of doing the same thing, over and over again.

Disadvantages

It can get lonely

When you are a freelance writer you are very much on your own and unless you are in touch with other freelance writers, it can get very lonely, particularly when you've secured a new commission and have no one to celebrate it with, or you've had a rejection letter telling you that an editor doesn't want your work. Writing is a very isolated occupation and not something that you can really do as part of a team, so you have to have a lot of faith in yourself and your abilities.

Rejection is part of the job

This is something that many new freelancers find very difficult to grasp and is often the main reason that makes them change their mind about wanting to be a freelance writer. You need to know right from the start that rejection is part and parcel of being a writer and learn early on that it's not personal. There are many reasons why an editor doesn't accept a piece of work (see the section on how to handle rejection) and you just have to accept this if you want to succeed. When you are first starting out, you will get more rejections than acceptances, but perseverance is the key and the more experience you get, the more likely you are to get a commission. Even the most proficient freelancer gets rejected on a weekly basis.

Procrastination

This is one of the most common problems of being a freelance writer and you will be surprised at how appealing the idea of washing the car is at times when you really should be chasing work! In fact, it has taken me three days to start writing this book! The problem with putting things off is that you end up getting nothing productive done. If you are going to work as a freelancer, you are responsible for securing your own work. It's a whole different ball-game to working for someone else. If you don't secure regular commissions, you don't get paid. Simple as that. There's truth in the saying that in order to succeed in anything you have to put in the time. You can't dig a hole just by having a shovel in your hand. You have to actually dig! Likewise, you won't become a freelance writer just by having a keyboard in front of you. At some point you will have to sit down and type!

You are responsible for getting work

Until it is established that you are a good freelancer to work with, it is up to you whether you get any work or not. It's up to you to make sure you commit at least one day a week to pitch to editors, make enquires and keep up to date with editorial changes. Work doesn't come flooding in just because you have a letterhead and a business card. Some weeks you will pitch several ideas and not even get a reply from anyone, let alone a commission. It happens, but if your aim is to be in the position where editors contact you, you have to start somewhere and put the hours in.

Now that we have covered some advantages and disadvantages of life as a freelance writer, we will look more closely at what it means to be a freelance writer...

What You Need to Be a Freelance Writer

To be honest with you, you can write anywhere: you don't necessarily have to have the latest Mac and an office the size of a penthouse. If you have a pencil and a notebook, you can work from your kitchen table, if you so wish, but in this day and age, when editors expect their writers to email submissions, and present their work in a professional way, it pays to at least have a computer with reliable Internet access. Below is a list of things you should consider investing in if you are going to succeed as a freelance writer:

- A good quality PC or laptop
- A printer
- 80gm and 100gm paper
- A selection of pens and pencils
- Stamps
- A selection of notebooks
- Two accounts books – one for income the other for expenses
- A calculator
- Paperclips
- A selection of reference books, including a thesaurus and a dictionary
- A mobile phone
- An email address
- A website to showcase your work or let editors know about you
- A diary
- Writeable CDs
- Several USB memory sticks (always save your work!)
- A selection of envelopes
- A current copy of *The Writers' and Artists' Yearbook*

- An area where you can work undisturbed
- An address book or an index card system

Whilst these 20 items won't necessarily make you a good writer (although the spell-checker is often a life saver!) they will help you well on the way to becoming a professional and being taken seriously by editors and publishers.

Of all the freelance writers I know, every one of them has a genuine interest in the written word. This is always a bonus. If your work is littered with grammatical errors or punctuation and spelling mistakes, work will dry up pretty quickly and you won't last very long as a freelance writer. Many people who decide to become writers find they are attracted to the idea because they may have had to do some form of writing in their previous line of work, such as writing up reports or the in-house newsletter, but it pays to take a refresher course in basic punctuation and grammar prior to sending work out for publication.

Freelance writing is a very competitive business and you will be competing with other professionals, so it's worth being the best you can be and learning as much as you possibly can about the business you will be in, because you can be sure that every other freelancer has done their homework before starting their business.

Writing's a Business – So Treat it as Such

Whether you write novels, non-fiction books, articles, screenplays, poems or even joke books, if you want to write for a living, by which I mean earn a good income from it, then you need to treat it as a business.

You may think that the piece you've just written is worthy of the Man Booker Prize, but if it's not commercially viable, then no one is going to buy it. It sounds harsh, I know, but if you want to be paid to write, then you need to make sure that what you write is going to be of some benefit to a reader – knowledge or entertainment or both. It also pays to take a completely objective look at your writing and ask yourself: would I be willing to use my own hard-earned money to publish this? If the answer is no, then can you really expect someone else to?

This is why I always say to up and coming writers that you should consider writing as you would any other business. If you are hoping to sell your writing, then you need to persuade an editor, a publisher or a producer that your work is worthy of their money. So how do you do this?

Basically, publishing, in whatever form, is a business: if you were the editor of a magazine, you would want to make sure that the article you were paying £400 for was going to attract more readers to your magazine, right? If you were a publisher of non-fiction books, you would want to know that the subject you are publishing is going to give you a return of at least triple the amount you paid out (the advance to the writer). If you were a producer, you would want to be 100% sure that the script you commissioned had a good chance of being a box office hit and would make a good return on your investment.

The good news for a writer is that there will always be people thirsty for knowledge and entertainment and willing to part with their hard-earned cash, whether that is for a book, a play, a movie or a magazine/newspaper.

However, the secret and often the hardest part in securing publication is to find a unique angle to promote whatever it is you are trying to sell. For example, in every women's magazine, every summer, you will find the same subjects: Safety in the Sun, Bikini Diets, Best Places to Go On Holiday, etc. Now, if you submit another how-to-get-into-your-bikini-in-two-weeks type of feature, it's more than likely that you will get a thanks, but no thanks. If, however, you presented them with a study of how good protective sunglasses really are, or how beneficial the sun really is for you, or the best things to do in the summer for free, then you could be looking at a commission.

They say there is no subject that hasn't already been written about; the art is in how you present the subject. There are many self-help books on the shelves of book shops, but if you presented a publisher with, say, a twenty-step plan to get your life in order, then you may just make a publisher pick up the phone and dial your number.

As much as I would love to say that thought-provoking literary works sell millions, they don't. Simple as that. What sells is commercial writing – in other words, writing that is going to appeal to as wide a range of people as possible. Just look at the *Purple Ronnie* poems by writer Giles Andreae: Andreae's rhyming poems and stick-figure drawings will never qualify for a top literary award, nor will he become poet laureate of the year, but they sell in their millions – in fact he sold the rights to *Purple Ronnie* two years ago for a staggering £4.8 million! So if you want to make money out of writing, then you need to get your business head on and write for a commercial audience, putting a unique angle on your pitch.

There are literally hundreds of stories in magazines and newspapers that you can expand on too: for example, when Prince William married Kate Middleton, the papers were full of the story of the royal wedding. You could interview other couples who got married on the same day, or you could write a piece on the most unusual proposals, unusual wedding dresses, the cheapest wedding, a short cut-out-and-keep filler on what gifts you should give for wedding anniversaries, a story about traditional gypsy weddings, or weddings from different cultures. From this one news item you could write several features or stories and an editor would be more likely to buy it from you because of the connection to the royal wedding.

A few months ago there was a story about an 80s pop star that had turned to alternative therapies to help cure him of his eczema. After reading this story, I sold a feature about using crystals for healing to the features editor of the same newspaper that ran the story.

If there is a story in the news, say for example, of a high-profile celebrity having a diva strop, perhaps you could write an item about how to handle people who often have diva moments, or a fun quiz about how to find out if you are a diva! Once you put your business head on and start to think of your writing as a business, you will find that you attract a lot more commissions.

Qualifications

One of the questions I am asked on a regular basis is: do you have to be a qualified journalist or have an MBA in creative writing in order to become a professional writer?

Although I did train as a journalist, in short the answer is no, and here's why...

Unless you are applying for a staff job or an internship on a newspaper or a magazine, you don't actually need to have any journalism qualifications. What you do need is a good, basic grasp of the English language, the ability to come up with good, saleable ideas, be able to deliver your copy on time and work to editors' briefs without kicking up a fuss.

Prior to writing for a living, I worked in numerous jobs – as a PA, a vet's assistant, in a travel agent, stuffing teddy bears to be sold in Harrods, to name but a few. I didn't start writing with a view to earning an income until I was 28 and decided to take a diploma in journalism. Whilst this was a good introduction to how writing for the media worked, I learned more by trial and error than any module could have taught me.

Writing to the standard where editors contact you, rather than having to chase them yourself, only comes from experience. The more you pitch, the more you learn what a particular editor likes and dislikes, and the more you study the market you are aiming to write for, the more likely you are to secure commissions. It doesn't matter to an editor whether you have a Masters in journalism, a handful of qualifications or even no qualifications. What matters is that you can write in the same style as the rest of their publication and can offer something their readers want to read about. So don't worry if you have no or few qualifications, it really doesn't matter. But where do you start?

Writing for Magazines – Where to Start...

You only have to look in any newsagents to see the vast amount of magazine titles available on every subject you can think of, which is always good news if you are a freelance writer, but how do you get to the stage where editors are contacting you and requesting features from you?

The easiest and best way to start out on a career in freelance writing is to begin with letter writing. Now I know many of you will be shouting, 'But I want to write features, now!' You need to trust me on this one. Writing letters to a magazine gives you a whole host of skills that you will need when you begin freelancing proper.

First and foremost, writing letters to magazines will give you good training in working out the style, the content and the readership of any given title. For example, *Woman's Weekly UK* – if you study the letters page in this magazine you will notice that the majority of readers are a) female, b) aged between 40 and 65 and c) concerned about everything from what to wear to a wedding to funny things their grandchildren have said. This gives you a good idea of what your target audience is. Furthermore, if you have a good look through the magazine, you will see the range of subjects that is covered, from natural health to the best kitchen appliances to buy. Another clue to the readership of a magazine is in the advertising pages at the back. Again, this gives you a good idea of who is going to read this particular magazine. If these pages are advertising cosmetic surgery, you know that the audience for that magazine is women who are concerned about their looks and can afford to change their looks by cosmetic surgery. If the magazine you are intending to write for is advertising stair-lifts, you know that it is aimed at an older audience.

I always advise people to read at least three back copies of any publication they are hoping to write for. This will give you a good idea of what an editor is looking for, especially for their 'Star Letter'.

Editors that I work for tell me that they like letters that refer to a previous issue and anything that praises the magazine, tips that could help other readers in some way, or reference to a previous feature that has helped the reader.

The best magazines to aim for are the cash-paying ones. It's all very nice to receive a bunch of flowers or a crystal vase, but as we are trying to earn money from writing, go for the magazines that pay cash for letters, tips, funny photos, etc. The big payers are what I call the real-life-story mags, such as the UK's *Take a Break*, *Chat*, *Love It*, *Pick Me Up*, etc. I know several writers who make a good living from just writing letters to magazines, but we are using this method of writing as a step up to writing full features.

When writing a letter to a magazine, always write it by hand and on some nice writing paper. If you send in a typed letter, an editor may think that you have sent a duplicate letter to every magazine in the industry. It's much nicer and more authentic if you send a letter that has some reference to the individual magazine you are targeting, so don't try to make a quick buck by sending the same, 'I love your mag!' letter to every editor. They won't print it.

Once you have a few published letters under your belt and hopefully a bit of extra cash, you can then start thinking about writing bigger pieces, such as fillers, which we will look at next.

As you get more into freelance writing, you will soon discover that the pieces that get accepted will be the ones on subjects that you are most passionate about. This will give you a good idea as to what to write about next. If for example you've had an article or two about healthy cooking accepted, it is an indication that this is a subject that not only interests you, but that you also write about well.

From this you can then think about specialising. The good

thing about specialising in a subject is that you soon become an authority on it and this is when editors contact you directly and ask for a specific piece, because they know that you are clued-up about the subject. The more you can specialise, the more you can aim your pitches to a specific market. However, it's also worth pointing out here that if you specialise too much, you could limit your potential income.

Personally, I've written articles that come under the genre of 'general lifestyle', but because I've always been interested in spiritual and alternative lifestyle features, and have had several books published in this genre, I tend to slide more towards those publications that cover that type of subject. I've been lucky enough to have written for every mind, body and spirit magazine on the market and have even written about MBS subjects for national newspapers. I'm on very good terms with all the editors I work with and I now get messages in my inbox saying things like, 'Debs, do you know anything about pyromagic and if so can you write 1400 words on it for me, please?'

So if you're looking for regular work, think about what you can specialise in, then look around to see what markets are out there that match your skills, knowledge and interests.

Filling in the Blanks

Readers' Letters is not the only market for people starting out in freelance writing. Fillers or breakers, as they are sometimes known, are always required by editors of magazines and newspapers. Fillers are those little snippets of interesting information that you often see at the bottom of a feature and do just what they say – fill space.

Fillers can be on any subject and are usually around the 400-500 word mark. They don't necessarily have to have any connection with the article they are filling and they pay well too, ranging from £100 to £350 for 500 words. I've written fillers on all manner of subjects, from little-known facts about Elvis to how nursery rhymes came about.

Most magazines and newspaper supplements carry fillers or breakers and the weekly publications are the best ones to target because they have to try to keep bringing in fresh material on a weekly basis.

So, what should you write about and how do you get an editor interested enough to commission you to write their fillers? Anniversaries are always a good place to start, but not your usual x-amount-of-years-since-the-death-of-Princess-Diana... There are many date-related websites such as http://www.ideas4writers .co.uk/books/date-a-base/index10.htm that offer a downloadable book of dates for the year of different anniversaries for a couple of pounds.

Think of unusual things or everyday items that we use in our daily lives, then research when they were invented. For example, 60 years ago this September, the first ever automatic telephone answering machine was tested. From this snippet of information you can write a good filler of facts relating to answering machines, such as the longest message left on one, the funniest message recorded, etc.

Another idea for fillers is items that are news related. A recent story in the press was of a famous celebrity apologising for inappropriate behaviour at a celebrity bash. A colleague of mine wrote a filler on five easy ways to apologise to someone.

Fillers can be on anything and everything. For instance, special occasions: how many greeting cards are sold in this country? What percentage of men to women buy greeting cards? How many Valentine's cards are sold every year? Household accidents: how many accidents-by-ironing-board are reported each year? See, anything and everything can be made into an interesting filler. If you have a knack for trivia, you may even get a regular column from it!

When you approach an editor with an idea, always, always find out the name of who you should contact. This is easily done by phoning the magazine/newspaper direct and asking. Nowadays many editors will accept email submissions, but do go careful if you have a hotmail, or other free email address. Many media offices automatically reject mail coming from these addresses for fear of being sent computer viruses.

If you have an idea for a filler, write a brief paragraph to your contact, along the lines of...

Stewart Jones

Did you know that a cow gives nearly 200,000 glasses of milk in her lifetime? Or that a woodpecker can peck twenty times a second? To coincide with World Animal Day on xxx, I wondered whether you might be interested in a 500-word filler of little-known trivia about animals?

I would be happy to email my copy over to you if you are interested. Thank you for your time.

Regards
A Writer

A point to note here is that you should never send attachments to an editor. If you do you will not get a reply because they will not open your email. Always ask first.

As with any submissions it is trial and error – some publications may need fillers, others may not, but if you don't try you'll never know.

Writing What You Know

Writers of fiction are often advised to write about what they know. Why? Simply because it's a whole lot easier than writing about a subject they know little or nothing about, not to mention the amount of research you have to do on an unknown subject.

The same applies with writing non-fiction. Whether it be a book or an article, it is so much easier if you know something about your subject, than if you were to pluck a subject out of the air, research it, and write about it as if you are an expert. Because that is what readers want – information from someone who knows more than they do on a certain subject. There's little point in telling your reader something they all ready know about – and little chance an editor will run a feature like that. Specialise in something you can share; whether it's IT skills, being able to cook a family meal in under 10 minutes, or household cleaning tips; there will always be something that you know or a skill that you have that other people would like to know about, and more importantly a publication that will be willing to print it.

I always advise people starting out in freelance writing to buy a current copy of *The Writers' and Artists' Yearbook* or *The Writers' Handbook*. These are the writers' bibles and list, among other things, every magazine and newspaper published in the UK, and many overseas, including editorial contacts, what they publish, what they are looking for and what rates they pay. A quick look through will reveal that there is a publication for almost every hobby, interest or occupation, from Accountancy Age to Zoo Magazine and everything in between.

Most of us when asked what our fields of expertise are, will shrug and assume that we don't know anything of use that we can pass on to other people. But when you start thinking about it, you will soon see that there are many things that you have either experienced or know about that you can elaborate on:

For example: leaving home, passing your driving test, owning a pet, moving in with someone, breaking up with someone, having a baby, attending an interview, securing a job, travelling around the world on a donkey, running a family on a budget, death, blogging, sending an email, holding a children's party, cleaning tips, reviewing books/DVDs etc, complaining, fashion, shoes...

I could go on, but this gives you an idea. Think back to all the experiences you've ever had and draw on these for inspiration. Draw up a list of everything you know about; even if it seems silly and obvious to you, there will always be a market to write about it.

Now You Have an Idea

OK, so by now you should be full of ideas, or at least have one that you can write about. You should also have some idea of who you are going to pitch it to. Obviously if it's something along the lines of Goat Herding the Easy Way, then your market to pitch is going to be a lot smaller than say, Five Meals for Under a Fiver, but you will be surprised at what some magazines will publish given a good enough angle. If you were a mother of three and decided to take a year off to learn how to herd goats in Nepal, an editor of a woman's lifestyle magazine would be interested in this kind of 'grown-up-gap-year' story. In fact I've just discovered a website dedicated entirely to goat farming in Nepal, if anyone is interested.

And here is the crucial part – the angle. The angle or the 'hook' as it is sometimes referred to is what will get your foot in the door, or email in the inbox of a features editor. If you have an interesting angle you are halfway there and the best way of getting that angle is (as I have pointed out earlier) to read previous but recent copies of the magazine and look at the headlines. For example, you may have a natural talent for surfing the Internet. If you were to pitch this to the editor of say *Saga* magazine, your angle could be something like...'Getting Down with the Kids – How to Keep in Touch with Your Modern Grandchildren', detailing how to email, send and receive photos and join Facebook, etc. If you were to approach a magazine aimed at busy mums, the angle could be...'Surf and Save Time and Money', highlighting how readers can order goods online, check price comparisons and source free High Street shopping vouchers, etc. The same subject could be pitched to a younger audience about 'Surfing Safely on Networking Sites'. Or if you also have a passion for animals, how about a 'Vets Online' feature for an animal magazine, showing how and where to get information for different animals? So, from one subject we now have four very different angles.

I know of one freelance writer who tries to get at least 50 acceptances for any one subject – and he usually does!

In the next part I will tell you how to go about actually pitching your idea. For now, see how many different angles you can get from just one idea and make a list of the publications that you think might be interested in it.

Pitching to an Editor

OK, so hopefully you are now bursting with ideas of what you would like to write about and which magazines or newspapers you are going to target, and if you've taken my advice, you should have already read some back copies of the publication you intend to target.

Unfortunately there is no one fast rule when contacting editors with a pitch: some prefer a brief outline by email, others prefer the more traditional route of sending the full article to them by post, and it's only with experience that you will discover what each editor prefers. The majority of editors I deal with prefer me to pitch an idea by email and it is very rare these days that I will write a full feature and send it to them. The reason for this is that each and every publication has its own style, so whilst the idea might seem a good one, an editor will always want your feature to be written in a similar style to the rest of their publication. For example, you may have an idea about writing a recession-related feature on how to make your money go further. Whilst this subject would appeal to most publications (after all, we've all been hit one way or another with the recession), the way *The Times* would want it written would be very different compared to how a woman's weekly magazine would want it.

Added to this, some publications have a kind of hierarchy, so although there will be an editor, there may also be a features editor, a deputy editor, or a commissioning editor who will be in charge of commissioning features. The way to find out who you should approach first is to look at the front of a magazine (or in *The Writers' and Artists' Yearbook* for newspapers) where the editorial team will be listed. There should also be an editorial phone number, so you can always phone and ask the receptionist to give you the contact for feature enquiries.

There are only a few major players in the UK magazine publication world that produce most of the magazines you see on the High Street. These include IPC Media, Bauer, Aceville and Natmags. As long as you know the name of the correct editor you can easily find out their editorial contact details by looking up the publishing company which will list the relevant email address. For example, all IPC editors are always: first name, underscore, last name at IPCmedia.com, so any magazine that is produced by IPC (*Take a Break, Ideal Home, Essentials, Cycling Weekly, Horse and Hound, NME, Woman's Weekly,* etc) are all first name, underscore, last name @IPCmedia.com.

Once you have found out how an editor of a particular publication likes to be contacted, then it's time to write your pitch.

The most important thing to remember is that editors are very busy people. It's a bit of a misconception that they just sit in an office all day reading emails. Many of them have to write a fair amount of copy for their publication, or carry out interviews. They have to make sure that everything they have planned for that week's/month's copy will actually fit, among other things, so it is important when contacting an editor to be brief and specific. Below is a copy of a recent pitch I did for a woman's magazine I hadn't pitched to before:

Dear (name of Features Editor)

I was wondering if you are currently commissioning freelance writers and if so if you are interested in a feature about sleep? (It is Love Your Bed Week from 2nd - 8th August.)

According to a recent study, 45% of people suffer stress-related insomnia at some point in their lives. I thought readers might be interested in knowing how they can get a good night's sleep, with box outs of tips, facts etc.

I write lifestyle and health features regularly for most of the UK women's and health magazines and some of the national newspapers.

I look forward to hearing from you.

Best wishes
Deborah Durbin

It's short and to the point and this is what editors want (and yes, I did get a commission from this pitch). Editors don't want to know that your mum or friends think you're a brilliant writer, or that you read their publication every week without fail. If your pitch suits their publication and you can demonstrate that you are confident and know what you are talking about, you will get a commission.

Don't worry if you haven't had anything previously published – everyone has to start somewhere and this won't hinder your chances of publication. If you know your subject (see previous section about writing what you know!) you can just as easily convince an editor to commission you – in fact it is often easier to pitch about something you know about.

After I had written my book about Native American Astrology, I found it very easy to get commissions on this subject because I already had knowledge and experience of it. I even got a column out of it for a national magazine. So don't think just because you haven't written for publication before you don't stand a chance – you do. Editors always want fresh material.

Another point to make here is one of timing: most monthly magazines will be planning their pre-Christmas issues from August, so pitching a 'bikini-diet' feature in July will be of no use to any weekly publication. In August I am pitching New Year ideas for monthly magazines!

Finally here are some Do's and Don'ts when pitching to an editor:

DO
· Be polite but to the point
· Be prepared to change your idea to suit the publication

- Contact the right person – or you may find you go through to the advertising department and end up buying a box ad!
- Be prepared to meet deadlines
- Leave your contact details

DON'T

- Say how fabulous you think the publication is – no one likes a suck-up!
- Refuse to budge on your idea
- Tell the editor what is missing from their publication or what they are doing wrong
- Miss deadlines – you won't be commissioned again
- Feel bad about rejection and send the editor hate mail!
- Ask them their rates of pay!

Next I will talk about payment and whether it's ever a good idea to write for nothing, and also show you how to deal with rejections (because trust me, you will get them!).

Payments, Rejections
and All That Malarkey

OK, so if you're still reading this then I'm assuming that you're still interested in writing for a living – either that or you're a loyal member of my family. Freelance writers can earn vast amounts of money, particularly if they specialise in something. Freelance writers can also go for long periods where they earn nothing or very little; that's the life of a freelancer, I'm afraid – feast or famine. However, even the most established freelancers had to start somewhere and build up a portfolio of clippings and will very often write a number of features for no payment, particularly if they want to be featured in a high-profile or prestigious magazine or newspaper.

Now, I know this book is all about writing for a living – as in earning money for what you write, but it often pays in the long run for a freelance writer to offer their work for nothing more than a credit or a byline. The important thing to remember here is how a magazine or newspaper works. All editors, regardless of how big their publication is, will have a budget from which they are able to commission their freelance writers. Some of these budgets are big, most are small in relation to the editor's desire to fill the pages with as much information for the reader as possible. You may offer a fabulous idea to an editor, but their budget might not stretch to paying for another commission, regardless of how much an editor likes your pitch. Magazines in particular rely heavily on advertising, so if an editor has the choice between a feature or a full-page ad they are going to take the ad.

You have two choices here – pitch your article to another publication or offer it to the first editor for free. If you decide to pitch it to another editor and make a sale, great. However, if you offer it to the first editor, chances are he/she will remember you the next time you offer another feature and offer you payment for it. There are many writers that claim they are just like any other professional and that they should never expect to give their work away for nothing. Well, I'm afraid life's not as simple as that. If you have this attitude you may just find that in times of recession your work will completely dry up. If you can show a bit of give and take you will reap the rewards in the long term.

A few years ago I contacted the editor of a monthly women's magazine with a feature idea and asked if she was interested in it. She told me she loved it, but unfortunately her budget was used up for the rest of the year with regular items. I decided to offer it along with another two features for no payment in the hope that her freelance budget would increase at some point and that she would pay me something in the future. The gamble paid off and I now get a commission every time I sub a new feature to her. Not only does this put you in good favour with editors, it also builds up a nice portfolio of work for you to present to other editors when you are pitching ideas. So if you find a publication is interested but can't pay you at the moment, always consider letting them have it in return for a credit or a byline – it will pay you to do so in the long run.

Rates of pay vary from publication to publication. To give you a rough idea of what you can expect to earn you should take a look at the National Union of Journalists rates of pay, see http://media.gn.apc.org/rates/w1000mag.html

Magazines and newspapers pay either a basic fee or more often than not a fee per 1000 words. This can range from around £100 per 1000 words and upwards. Newspapers often pay the most. At the time of writing, *Take A Break* magazine in the UK pays £450 for 600 words, *Woman* magazine pays £450 for 900 words for First British Serial Rights (I will talk about rights in a bit) and *The Daily Express* Saturday Magazine pays £600 for a feature, so it's well worth writing for the newspaper and magazine market.

I also want to talk about rejection in this section. Rejection is something that every freelancer faces on a daily basis and something that you will have to get used to if you wish to make a living as a freelance writer. The main thing to remember is that it is not personal; it is just part of the job. There is a lot of competition from freelance writers, so when an editor tells you they are already running a similar feature, they are not lying to you, they really are running a similar feature. In fact, to get a reply from an editor is a great accomplishment! More often than not you will not even get a reply.

Just because one editor doesn't commission you, it doesn't mean another won't. Just resubmit it to someone else. Expect that for every 10 submissions you might get one commission, so be prepared to keep subbing and don't be put off just because an editor says no thanks. Try again and again and again if necessary. Persistence is the key to freelance writing!

Rights

In this section I'm going to talk about publishing rights, what they are and how to protect yourself and your work. Whenever you write something, by law you always retain the copyright to your work, unless of course you give away or sell that right in the form of All Rights Including Copyright or Exclusive Rights Including Copyright (which is never advisable), which in layman terms basically means that whoever has paid for those rights has ownership of your words and you hand over all control of your article or book. It also means you cannot re-sell that work again.

Most magazines and newspapers ask for or expect First Serial Rights. This gives that particular publication exclusive rights to publish your feature in a magazine, newspaper, book, etc. If you are subbing to a British publication, for example, they often term it as First British Serial Rights (FBSR), which means you are allowing that particular British publication first rights to publish your feature, so you can't sell *exactly* the same feature to another British publication.

If another publication is also interested in running the same feature, you can sell them Second Serial Rights. Obviously you will not get as much money for selling Second Rights, but it does mean you can re-sell the *exact* same feature over and over again to different publications.

Then we have One Time Rights. One Time Rights gives a publication the right to print your work only once – so they couldn't reprint your feature year in year out, which is what some publications do.

There are also Electronic Rights. This grants a publisher the rights to publish your work on the Internet, or in some other electronic form such as a CD or an eBook.

Syndication Rights are when the author gives a syndicate agency the right to sell a feature over and over again to various publications, for a commission per sale. This is often used for freelancers who specialise in writing about celebrities or world events.

Finally back to All Rights: I would never advise a writer to sell All Rights to their work. It means that your work becomes the property of whoever buys it. It also means that they can then re-sell it, again and again and again, in any format they choose, so you can never re-sell it as your work. Many online article companies do this.

As I mentioned earlier, there is nothing to stop you from selling a feature based on the same subject to a number of different publications. Obviously you won't win any favours by selling the *exact* same content to different editors, but it's certainly acceptable to sell the same subject matter, just written in a different way to suit different magazines and newspapers. Or, of course you can also sell the exact same feature by offering Second Serial Rights, or by taking a percentage from a syndication agency.

Next I will talk about how to format your feature/article properly to meet industry standards.

Structure and Style

When you have your idea mapped out and have hopefully made a successful pitch, it's time to think about the structure and style of your article. For those who have never submitted an article to an editor, there are some specific industry standards you should adhere to if you are going to impress an editor and look professional.

Font: You should always type your manuscript in a simple font, such as Times New Roman or Arial and it should always be printed in black. Swirly fonts and pretty colours will not impress the editor. They are too hard on the eye to read and editors receive hundreds of submissions per week, so stick to a simple font and lose the temptation to pretty it all up!

Spacing: All manuscripts should be typed, set at double-lined spacing and justified to the left of the page. It's not up to you to typeset your feature – leave that to the professionals. What you should be thinking about is making your manuscript as easy to read as possible.

Punctuation and spelling: There is nothing more frustrating for an editor than trying to read a manuscript that is littered with spelling and punctuation mistakes. No sooner than they get into the feature than they have to stop to re-read a sentence that doesn't make sense. Always double-check what you have written before submitting it and always print on only one side of the paper. If your feature goes over one A4 page, always remember to number your pages at the bottom right-hand corner. It pays to print out a copy and read it with fresh eyes. For some unknown reason we tend to miss obvious mistakes more on the screen than if we read a printed copy.

Beginning, middle and the end: You will remember from writing stories at school that they should always have a beginning, a middle and an end and non-fiction is no exception. Pick up any magazine or newspaper and you will see that every article has something in common – they all have a beginning, a middle and an ending. The beginning of your feature should always 'hook' the reader to make them want to read on. This is easily achieved with a bit of thought. For example, for a feature I was commissioned to write about eating well in the recession, I began the feature with, 'Just because we're in a recession it doesn't mean that we can't have a healthy diet. Here are the top ten super-foods that don't cost a fortune...' Always try to make your beginning as short as possible. An average sentence length for your hook should be no longer than about 30 words and should give the reader an idea of what they are going to read about next. Many freelancers include statistics in their hook, for example, 'According to a recent study, 12–15 million people in America have had a near-death experience...' This is a great hook that grabs the reader's attention and makes them want to read on. The middle of your article should contain the main information you want to get across. Always finish your feature with a good ending, tying up any loose ends or questions the reader may have.

Don't try to impress: Unless you are writing for an academic journal, don't try to impress the editor or your potential reader with your knowledge of words. You may well know what bromidrosis is, but your readers don't want to have to keep referring to the dictionary to get the gist of what you're writing about! Always write in plain English. It won't impress anyone, particularly a commissioning editor, if you try to blind them with science.

Keep to the word count: Another annoying thing that editors don't like is when they ask you for a certain number of words and you don't keep to the word count. As a general rule most one-page features are between 800 and 1000 words. A double-page spread (DPS) can often be between 2500–3000 words. There is a reason why an editor requests a specific amount of words and that is because they have to make space for many more features, regular columns and advertising, so always, always adhere to the word count.

Box outs: Most magazine features have what are known as box outs. These are those little boxes of information at the side of the page relating to the subject matter in the article. If the magazine you are pitching to usually prints box outs, suggest one for your feature. These are often full of facts about the subject you are writing about and are usually bulleted points of information. For example, I wrote an article on how having a pet can be healthy for you and the editor wanted three box outs about people who had been saved by their pets. A quick search on the Internet led me to the stories I needed.

Always deliver on time: Once you are commissioned to write a piece for publication you will be given a deadline to work to. This is because the publication has to go to print on a certain date and requires all copy to be in so that it can be edited, designed and typeset prior to printing. You should always stick to your deadline if you want further work from that editor.

What to Say...and What Not to Say...

I've been in the writing business for 15 years now and have also been on the other side of the fence as an editor, so I've picked up a few pointers along the way as to what to say and what not to say when contacting an editor for freelance work, so I thought it might be helpful to share them here...

DO

Be professional: The majority of editors prefer to be contacted by email nowadays, but there is always the exception. Either way, whenever you contact an editor always act professionally. By this I mean, if you are writing a query, make sure you know the name of the editor. Don't ever write 'Dear Editor' in a pitch. If you are subbing by email, make sure you have a professional email address. Tweetypie@hotmail.com doesn't look very professional when you're trying to impress an editor!

Make your subject interesting: Every editor dreams of an easy life and if you can deliver a pitch that explains exactly what you plan to write about, then this makes the editor's job a lot easier. A vague, 'I thought you might like something about blogging' is a bit, well, vague. But what if you said, 'Did you know that there are an estimated 70 million blogs out there in cyberspace and 247 million emails are sent around the world every day? Is the Internet taking over our lives?' This will make an editor think, wow! Is that 247 million? By being more specific you are more likely to get a commission.

Know the publication: I know it's a bit of a pain to buy and read several back copies of a publication you would like to write for, but if you study a publication you will easily recoup the amount you spend on issues tenfold. Every publication has its own style and readership, so it really is worth paying attention to this. There is no point writing a how-to-get-a-hot-date article aimed at the twenty-something market and sending it to *The People's Friend* and vice versa, a feature about the memoirs of a seaside town wouldn't go down well with the editor of say, *Cosmopolitan*. It seems as if I'm stating the obvious but you would be amazed at the amount of times this happens.

Be honest: If you extend the truth and say that you can get an interview with Angelina Jolie, get a commission and then don't deliver, you won't be asked to write another article for that publication again. If you find you can't make a deadline, be honest and tell the editor. There is nothing worse than planning a page only to find that the writer you've commissioned can't deliver the work. Editors are people too and do understand that sometimes life gets in the way of deadlines.

Leave the editing to the editor: It doesn't matter how perfect you think your copy is, it is an editor's right to cut and edit where they think they need to. Most magazines and newspapers rely heavily on advertising to generate revenue, so the features department are always, always short of space and features do have to get cut from time to time. An editor may well cut the best parts out of your copy, but don't throw a fit and reprimand them. They know their publication inside out, so leave the editing to the editor.

Make sure editors can find you: A website or a blog can cost nothing but time to set up, so get one and make it look as professional as you can. You can buy a domain name for as little as £7 per year, which is a very worthwhile investment. A website will act as your virtual CV: once you have one you can add lists of publications you've worked for, samples of your work, chapters of your books and information about yourself. This will be your one-stop-shop for editors to find out all about you. Just don't be tempted to add photos of your family, pet dog or auntie Dot. I'm sure Auntie Dot would be thrilled but it doesn't look very professional. Save that for Facebook.

DON'T

Be OTT friendly: An editor may well be impressed with you and say nice things about your work, but don't assume that this means that you are Best Friends Forever and start every email with endearing words such as, 'Hiya Sweetie!' or 'How's it hanging?' Keep your friends and your editors separate. You are a professional, so always act like one. No matter how nice an editor is to you, the minute you get too familiar is the minute they will think you're a bit weird and will back away from you.

Assume an editor will take everything you pitch: Just because you've had a good run of features with one publication, don't assume that you can put your feet up and that now this editor will want anything you throw at him/her. Publications change as do editorial desks – all the time. You may offer something similar to what they have already commissioned from another freelancer, or a big news item might surface and your item gets dropped. It's nothing personal. It's life.

Attack an editor – ever! If you do you will find it very hard to gain freelance work again. Remember there are only three or four major publishing companies in the magazine industry in the UK and word does get round. Whether an editor sends you a curt 'no thanks' or your commission has been dropped in favour of something else, take it in your stride. Do not fire off a 'You're nothing but a *&^%$*!!!' reply. It will do you no favours. Go and have a rant in the garden instead.

Accuse an editor of stealing your idea: Yes, it does occasionally happen; you pitch a good idea, have it turned down, only to find it in the next publication, written by a staff-writer. Again, this is something that goes with the job. It can simply be a coincidence, but even if you've had a winner of an idea and an editor thinks one of their in-house staff can write the copy, ideas are not protected by copyright. Shrug and move on. You can always sell your idea to someone else, but if you accuse an editor of stealing your idea, you will never get work from him/her again.

Don't undersell yourself: Pitches starting with, 'I hope you don't mind me bothering you,' or 'I'm sure you're not interested, but I thought I would try anyway,' are never good. Remember, editors have a budget and you are a writer wishing to earn an income from your writing. Editors want the best copy they can get and are prepared to pay for it. Treat it like a business transaction. If you don't feel your writing is worthy of payment, then neither will an editor. Be professional and you will get treated in the same way.

Send attachments: Editors a) don't have time to open attachments and b) don't like to open attachments in case they open something containing a computer virus. Always email first with a query. If they are interested they will either send you a brief with a word count, deadline, etc, or will ask you to send them some samples as an attachment. Or they may commission you there and then.

Embarrass yourself online: In this age where anyone and everyone has a Facebook or Twitter account you can easily get carried away with delivering far too much information on the Internet. You think it's hilarious to post a photo of yourself at a party, too much the worse for wear, but is this really the image you want to portray to potential editors? Editors go online too, you know. They also know how to work Twitter and Facebook and might also belong to online writers' forums. Remember these words: make sure that whatever you write on the Internet is something that you don't mind the whole world knowing about!

News-worthy?

Writing for newspapers is one of the most profitable areas a freelance writer can get into. They have big commission budgets (articles can pay anything from a few hundred pounds to a few thousand, if you have a celebrity scoop) and because the nationals are produced on a daily basis, there is a need for good, news-worthy copy every day. Now, there's a clue in that sentence – *news-worthy*!

Newspapers sell *news* and this is why a lot of freelancers find it challenging to break in to newspaper work. They supply features that are just that, features, and whilst some of the daily newspapers do run general features, these are usually done in-house by staff-writers. After all, why pay a freelancer for something that a staff-writer can knock out? However, if you can learn to put a news angle on a subject you will have a very lucrative career in newspapers.

A few years go I did an interview with a best-selling romance novelist. She had a new book coming out at the time and I was sure I could get her into one of the nationals. I approached a couple of editors I'd worked for before and was asked, 'What's the news angle?' 'Well, she has a new romance book out,' I offered. 'Does she feel she has to write romance because she's unlucky in love?' my editor asked. 'Errr, no, she's happily married,' I replied. 'OK, has she got a terminal illness?' 'I don't think so, she didn't say,' was my response.

Do you see where this is going? It wasn't enough that this lady had a new book out. The newspapers wanted something news-worthy if they were going to run this story.

Writing for newspapers is very different to writing for magazines and you have to constantly ask yourself, what's the news angle on this? It is possible to turn any subject into a news-worthy topic, as long as you keep up to date with what is going on in the world, which is why I constantly tell writers to read as many newspapers, from the red-top tabloids to the broadsheets, as they possibly can. All newspapers want to run interesting but at the same time news-related articles for their readers, so it's important to keep up with what's been happening in the news and act quickly if you want to secure a commission.

Recently, for example, newspapers have been inundated with the news of super injunctions for celebrities, politicians and sports stars. Despite what you may think about them (and this is another important aspect of writing for newspapers – you must be unbiased at all times), there are several news features that can be bounced off of this subject: you could interview a judge or a lawyer that opposes super injunctions. With the news that a member of a popular social network leaked the names of some people who had super injunctions, you could question how safe social networks really are, or perhaps how important they are for people who are house-bound, or how modern technology is taking over our social lives, or how staying in with your 'friends' on Facebook is the new going out.

A colleague of mine read an interview about a celebrity and his passion for adopting farm animals and contacted the editor of the national with a piece about her desire to keep urban chickens. The paper did a two-page spread on how she coped, from putting together a hen-house to rearing 10 chickens in her back garden.

As long as your item is linked to something that has been in the news and you can put a news angle on it, a newspaper editor will be willing to commission you.

Another idea for newspapers is anniversaries: last year I sold an item about tarot cards to a national on the basis that the Rider Waite Tarot Deck (the most famous tarot deck) was 100 years old. I bounced that idea after reading an item earlier in the week about a nightclub that was offering tarot readings to their clubbers.

And remember, all newspapers carry their own sections such as health, careers, finance, etc, so if you see, for example, a story about a particular business booming, you could pitch an item about how to start your own business. If a film is heavily publicised, for example, *The King's Speech*, you could write an item about speech impediments. Just remember, you need to pitch quickly and you need to be news-worthy. If you can combine these two skills, you could earn a fortune contributing to newspapers.

It's important to remember the six rules of journalism when writing for newspapers:

Who, what, where, when, why and how

Good journalism always asks these five questions:

Who: is the story about?
What: happened or what's the story?
Where: did it happen?
When: did it take place?
Why: did it happen?
How: did it happen?

Make sure you can answer all these questions within your piece when you approach an editor of a newspaper.

Some Legal Aspects

Due to limited space I can't go into a great deal about the law and writing, but there are a few things you should be aware of when you are writing, particularly if you are writing for the news/magazine market.

Libel

If you write something about another person that is not true and that defames their character, for example that someone has committed a crime, you can be sued for defamation of character. Make sure you check and double-check that you have your facts right. It is not enough to think that your editor will check; they don't have time to do this for every story. It is your job to report the truth and you as the writer can get into trouble if your copy is found to be false.

Hearsay

Again it is important that you only present the facts of a story when you write about it. Someone suspected of murder may well be considered a bit odd and a loner by his neighbours, but that doesn't make him a murderer. Don't listen to the gossip. Many a newspaper has been sued on the grounds that one of their reporters has written gossip or hearsay in their report. Always stick to the facts.

Plagiarism

Always pay particular attention to the source of your research when writing an article. For example, if you are quoting someone in the medical profession, contact that person and ask permission to use their findings. Much of your research will be done via the Internet, but that still doesn't make it free to all. Anything that is put in writing, whether in a book, another article or someone's website, is protected by copyright. It takes a few minutes to make a phone call or send an email to ask permission to use someone else's work to back up your article and I have found that most people are only too happy to oblige.

Web findings

Most writers will do their research on the Internet, but go carefully; you can't always trust everything you read. The Wikipedia website, for example, has come under fire for providing information that is speculative or simply not true, so always double-check your research. If you report something that is simply not true, regardless of whether it has been reported as fact elsewhere, you and the publication you are writing for could be sued by the person.

Fair comment

Fair comment is when you are entitled to write about someone who is already in the public eye. However, whilst we are all entitled to our opinions in the form of a review or a column, this doesn't give you permission to write something about another person that is untrue. You may write that you don't like a particular author's latest book and the reason why, but you can't write that the author doesn't write her own books anyway, unless you have proof of that.

Public interest

There's a clue in those two words – in the interest of the public. Always try to remember this when reporting an item. It's not really in the public's interest that a celebrity is having a string of affairs. If on the other hand the celebrity in question has done something illegal, then this would be considered 'in the public's interest'. The problem we have, particularly with the tabloid press, is that many stories that are reported are printed for sensationalism rather than in the public's interest. Always ask yourself:

what is the public's interest in this story? Is it just sensation-alism?

Biographies

When you are writing about another person it is vital that you stick to the facts. Your opinion of another person doesn't count. If you write a biography about someone living or dead in a poor light, there is the danger that this person or one of their relatives will sue you for defamation of character. As with any form of reporting, you should always stick to the facts and have an unbiased opinion about the people involved.

Different Forms of Freelance Writing: Part I

ebooks

Aside from writing for newspapers and magazines, there is a whole host of other avenues in which you can secure paid work as a freelance writer, so for the next few sections I am going to cover a few of these, starting with writing eBooks.

According to the International Digital Publishing Forum, US eBook sales reached a record-breaking high this year with a 250% increase, with over $40 million in sales from eBooks. With the introduction of new electronic readers such as the Kindle and the Sony E Reader this is an ideal opportunity for freelance writers to explore.

An eBook is simply a book that is set in an electronic format rather than a book printed on paper and can be read either by downloading it to your PC or on a mobile reader, an iPod or an iPhone, and if publishing industry figures are to be believed, this is the way of the future. Although eBooks will never replace paperbacks, they will work alongside them, giving readers the opportunity to choose between a paper and an electronic format.

This is a similar scenario to music CDs and iPods – they both exist quite happily alongside each other and the majority of publishers now produce their books in both paperback and digital format.

The bonus for a freelance writer is that it is so much easier and quicker to set up an eBook – in fact the hardest part is writing the actual content. Studies on eBooks have found that whilst novels do well as an additional choice in an eBook format, they usually also have to be printed as paperbacks. However, if you are looking at writing non-fiction, the world is your electronic oyster and eBooks really are the way to go.

So, what to write about? Well, anything you feel like. EBooks work best for non-fiction because it's a format that people will happily download if they feel they are going to learn something new. Non-fiction books generally sell less than their fiction counterparts in paper form, but figures show they do exceedingly well as eBooks.

People want to know things; whether it's information about metaphysics or a book on how to handle teenagers, you all know something that someone else doesn't know. What about your job, for starters? You may think it's boring or that anyone can do it, but there are people out there who will pay good money to know how to do what you already know how to do. You may have experience of caring for a pet; again, other people interested in that particular animal will want to know how to care for it. You may be in retirement and be in the position of pursuing your hobby full-time – again, you can write about it and inform others. You could be great at crosswords – other puzzle enthusiasts would love to know your tips and hints. Have you ever taken a driving test? Given up smoking? Attended an interview? Moved house? Know how to set up a website? Know how to work a computer, even? Ridden a horse? Cooked a meal for 10 for under a fiver? Can you take wonderful photographs? Are you well travelled? Do you know the perfect way to get a baby to sleep? Do you know how to spot a fake Prada handbag? (There is an actual eBook about just this; in other words spotting counterfeit goods.) Anyway, you get the idea. There are hundreds of things you know that other people will want to know. I have a friend who is always winning competitions. She wrote a book about all the tricks she learned of being a competition winner and it sells well.

Like I said, the hardest part is writing your book, but if you have a passion for writing and a passion for your subject, this shouldn't be too much of a problem. Whereas the next stage of getting a book published would be either to spend months touting your manuscript to agents and publishing houses if you were going the traditional route for a paperback, or to self-publish it, with an eBook you simply format it in an electronic file (this is usually done by the eBook publisher and you can simply submit your work as a Word document), present it to an ePublisher and job done! You will then start earning royalties.

You will be in good company: Stephen King published some of his stories in eBook format. You can now publish your book for free on Amazon Kindle Direct and it will be selling within 24 hours.

I know writers who have written hundreds of eBooks on all manner of subjects and they receive better royalties than if they had produced them in paperback. It doesn't even have to be a book as such. Many eBooks are snippets of information such as a series of Grandma's recipes or humorous real stories about working at the checkout in Tesco. Typical royalties for a traditional paperback book, produced by a traditional publisher, are between 10 and 15% of net sales. Typical royalties for an eBook are between 60 and 70%, and many ePublishers will also offer a print version of your book if you want it, so it's well worth considering this as an option to earn money from freelance writing.

As with everything there are good ePublishers, bad ePublishers and even ugly ePublishers. A quick Google search revealed thousands of publishers of eBooks, so you have to do your homework and make sure you read any contracts prior to signing with a company. One of the better ones I have come across are Lulu, and Amazon Kindle Direct. They charge no fees and have fabulous forums if you have any questions on how to get your eBook published.

Think about your life in general. What skills or knowledge do you have that you could pass on to others? Don't think that you don't know anything of any value, because you do.

A quick look at the Amazon non-fiction charts for eBooks shows that there are many different books and subjects that are selling: *Confessions of a GP*, *Seven Habits of Highly Effective People*, several misery memoirs, a family's 8000-mile trip around Britain in a Vauxhall Astra, quite a few on the subject of attaining success and happiness, and a teacher's tales of classroom hell, to name a few.

I'm sure you can come up with some of your own ideas for a non-fiction book from your own life experiences.

Different Forms of Freelance Writing: Part II

Blogs

We've looked at writing eBooks as another string to the freelancer's bow, but have you ever considered blog writing? It is estimated there are 126 million blogs on the Internet and blogging is big business. As I said in the previous section about writing eBooks, there are millions of subjects that make interesting reading and you personally know hundreds of subjects that other people don't know and would like to learn something about.

Just as with writing an eBook, writing a blog can be very lucrative. Celebrity writer Perez Hilton makes an estimated £100,000 a month from his writings about celebrities. He has over four million page hits per month. Advertisers love him for this and this is how he generates so much income. The blog, Overheard in New York, receives no less than six million hits per month. Tree Hugger – which does pretty much what it says on the tin – is a blog dedicated to everything that is green and environmental, and was sold to Discovery for $10 million in 2007. So you can see that a bit of blog writing can lead to a very lucrative lifestyle if you want it to.

There are blogs for every subject you can think of: from someone's diary entry of life as a newly divorced woman to political ramblings about the state of the world, to how to convert to Buddhism. You name it, there will be a blog about it and the best thing is that it's easier to write than an eBook because you just write and add small chunks of text as and when you feel like.

So just how do you generate a full-time income from blog writing?

There are many ways to do just this, including:

- Google Adsense
- Affiliate Programmes with companies such as Amazon
- eBooks relating to your subject
- Private adverts

If you go to the site Problogger you can read more about how to generate income from your blog, but primarily your aim is to get people to visit your site, so you need to make your writing as interesting and appealing to as many people as possible. This is what potential advertisers will want to know about if they are going to pay to advertise through your blog.

As with anything if you want to be heard you have to shout, so it's a good idea to join as many social networks and other people's blogs that cover your blog subject as possible. Once you have started your blog (through sites like Blogger or Wordpress), whenever you post a comment on another person's blog, readers of that blog can click your name and your blog will come up.

Most blogging sites have a button you can click on that will tell you how many people have visited your site. People won't know about your blog unless you tell them, so whenever you send out an email, always put your blog address at the bottom on your email. Do a blog swap and ask other bloggers to give you a mention. Contact magazines or newspapers if there is something in the news about the subject you are writing about and mention your blog. Join websites and mention your blog. The more you mention it, the more people will click on it, read it and tell others.

I would love to say that my own particular blog has millions of readers and generates millions of pounds for me – unfortunately it doesn't! As much as I would love to ramble on all day about how to make money from freelance writing, my family, my menagerie of pets and my commissioned writing prevent me from doing so, and I have to do my blog in my 'spare' time. But that's not to say that at some point I won't be able to dedicate more time to it. I still get a few hundred hits per month from readers wanting to know more about how to earn money as a freelance writer.

Think about what it is you know and can pass on: this could be anything from how to start a playgroup to how to become a sports writer or it could just be your day to day ramblings about life.

Different Forms of Freelance Writing:
Part III

Real-life Stories

One very lucrative form of freelance writing is the real-life story market. There are many weekly magazines on sale that run nothing but real-life stories such as the UK's *Take a Break, Closer, Pick Me Up, Love It* and so on and so forth. If you don't mind writing about subjects such as, 'My Husband Ran off with a Goat Herder' – and yes, that really was a story – then you can make a very good living from selling these real-life gems to magazines and newspapers.

Now, obviously not all of us live interesting and bizarre lives involving goats or even the herding of them, so whilst you may have your own marital skeletons in your cupboard that you would like to share with the nation, you are never going to have enough of your own material to make a good, regular income from telling your own real-life stories, and even if you did, this is probably not the best career move if you want to be known as a professional freelance writer. You will only become known as someone who has led a very colourful life, rather than a good writer.

There are literally hundreds of opportunities to sell real-life stories on a weekly basis and if you are the kind of person who can talk to anyone, empathise with their story and have good interview skills, you can sell other people's stories to some of the highest-paying publications on the market.

You can find stories everywhere you look. A friend of mine who specialises in confessional and real-life stories (and can talk the hind leg off a donkey), often comes up with real-life stories in conversation at the school gates and always offers to get the story published. Earning around £400–£600 per piece, she pays her interviewee between £150–£200 for an interview. She has written about everything from miscarriages of justice to bizarre weddings and even poltergeists. The majority of her income as a freelance writer comes from this one source.

Other ways to get interviews is to do what a lot of journalists do and that is to advertise. Just type in 'real-life stories wanted' into Google and you will find there are many freelancers who are more than willing to write them up and sell them.

It's very important if you are going to write and sell real-life stories that you gain the trust of the person you are interviewing and that you are not easily shocked – magazines such as these want sensational stories, not the bog standard, 'My Wife Had an Affair'. Rather they want, 'My Wife Had an Affair with My Sister!' So as a reporter of a story such as this you need to be non-judgemental and trustworthy so that you will write the story the way it has been told.

People are much more open and confessional nowadays than they once were – you only have to watch day-time TV to see this; if it's not Jeremy Kyle, it's Jerry Springer or Judge Judy on the telly! So there is a great amount of work to be had out there if you are interested in writing this kind of story and getting paid very well for doing so.

Different Forms of Freelance Writing: Part IV

Ghost-writing

Another good earner for the freelancer is ghost-writing. I don't mean writing about ghosts and other such spooky things, or even writing for ghosts. By ghost-writing I mean writing books and articles on the behalf of other people.

The biggest British ghost-writer is Andrew Crofts who has ghost-written hundreds of books on behalf of other people, including celebrities. Two of his ghost-written books have been in the best-seller list at the same time. He is known in the industry as one of the best ghost-writers and is the one that most main publishers contact first when they need someone to write a book on the behalf of someone else.

Not all celebrity autobiographies are written by ghost-writers and not all ghost-writing jobs entail delving into the lives of the rich and famous. I have personally ghosted three different books. None I hasten to add have been celebrities and I have been asked to write them for one of two reasons: either because the person had a story they desperately wanted to tell but didn't have the required skills to turn it into a book, or because they simply didn't have the time to dedicate a year or more to writing their story. You will not get any glory or even see your name on the cover of the book, so it is not a job that is suited to someone with an ego. You have to be able to write as though you are the actual 'author', so there is no room for your own words. You have to remain completely professional and write only what the subject wants you to write. It doesn't matter if you like (although it does help) or dislike the person you are writing for, or even if you agree or disagree with the subject you are writing about. You are being hired to write – that is it. Also bear in mind that the majority of people that hire a ghost-writer will ask you for complete anonymity and it's highly likely that you will be asked to sign a confidentiality agreement.

So how do you get into ghost-writing? There are many different ways: I was lucky in that the people who asked me to write their books contacted me directly, via either my website or a freelancing company that I belong to, or one of my publishers has contacted me to write for them on behalf of someone else. Other ways are by contacting publishing companies directly or advertising your services as a ghost-writer with a freelance/copy-writing company. It's ideal to have some experience of writing, or at the very least some samples of your work, but there is also another opportunity and that is by talking to ordinary people.

Mention that you are a writer and you will invariably hear the words, 'I have a good idea for a book, I just don't have the time to write it.' This is your cue to offer to write the book for them. Ghost-writing always works well with real-life stories, war memoirs, interesting autobiographies or workbooks and business titles. Rarely are novels ghost-written unless a celebrity puts his or her name to one. Another exception is that the original author was famous and has died, leaving a story untold and this is when a ghost-writer is drafted in to finish the novel.

So how do you get paid for ghost-writing? There are two options: the first is that you are paid a set fee to write the book. This is good if your subject is unknown and he/she doesn't have an agent or a publisher lined up. How much you are likely to be paid depends on the length of the book. Many ghost-writers work on an hourly basis currently anywhere between £24 and £40 per hour. If your subject is a celebrity or is famous for something and you are being hired by a publisher or an agent, it's more likely that you will be paid a basic fee followed by royalties of 50/50 with the 'author' up to around the £50,000 mark, then royalties may drop by 10% for every additional £50,000 you earn from the sales of the book. Obviously, as regards how much you will earn, it depends on how famous the person is.

The reason many publishers use ghost-writers is because they can rely on them to deliver a manuscript on time and they know that a book will be of a publishable standard. So once you prove you can do this, you could be the next Andrew Crofts, writing for a whole host of celebrities.

Different Forms of Freelance Writing: Part V

Greeting Cards

I'm now going to talk about writing for an industry that is worth almost £1.47 billion – the greeting card industry. According to the Greeting Card Association's 2010 market report, there are over 800 publishers producing a staggering 1.5 billion greeting cards a year – and for every one of those cards, someone somewhere had to write the greetings inside of them.

If you have a flair for poetry or verse, or even if you can write humorous prose, you could be earning good money if you contact one of the greeting card publishers. The name of the publisher is always printed on the back of a greeting card, so it's worth spending a few hours in a greeting card shop with a little notebook, pretending to look for a card and jotting down the name of the publishers. Alternatively if you go to the Greeting Card Association's website, there is a whole list of greeting card publishers' names and contact details, and submission guidelines. If you can illustrate or can take a good photo with a digital camera, all the better.

Rates for verse can and do vary depending on the publisher and vary from around £50 for a simple one-liner, to £300–£500 for a longer verse. Good quality, high-resolution photos can generate anything in the region of £300 per image for exclusive rights. The bigger publishers of greeting cards such as Hallmark offer the highest rates, but they are hard to get in to. If you keep submitting, however, odds are that you will eventually get an acceptance.

Below is a little information from the Greeting Card Association's 2010 report:

- The average retail price of an everyday card in 2010 in the UK was £1.41.
- Everyday cards accounted for 71% of the market's value – accounting for £1.036 billion worth of retail sales in 2009.
- Christmas cards accounted for 45% of the volume with 678.9 million cards sold, and 18% of the value at £267.2 million (2008 festive period).
- Spring season sales were worth £150.2 million with a total of 86.4 million cards being sent for Valentine's Day, Mother's Day, Easter and Father's Day.
- Some £57.1 million was spent on Mother's Day cards last year, on 21.5 million cards.
- Valentine's Day came next at £42.3 million on 21.5 million cards and Father's Day at £36 million also on 21.5 million cards.

So, if you find it easy to write love poems or can write something appropriate for your mother a couple of times a month, then you could easily be drawing in a good income from your writing.

Different Forms of Freelance Writing: Part VI

So You Want to Be a Sports Writer?

Not only is John Metcalfe one of my best friends, he is also a very talented script-writer and sports writer. Here he has written a section for me on how you can make it in the world of sports-writing...

When my good friend Debs asked me to write this part I thought, 'Yeah, I'm up for that. How difficult can it be?'

However, now I have had a few days to think about it I realise it is not as straightforward as I first thought.

So, first of all to Debs; I hope we can still be friends. And to the rest of you – I hope I don't put you off writing for life.

To give you some background, I have always loved writing and always enjoyed sport yet it took me until around the age of 28 to realise I could marry the two and forge a career for myself.

I was living in Stratford Upon Avon and noticed an advert in the local free paper that said, 'Do you read sports reports? Do you think you can do better?'

The proverbial light bulb went off in my head and I applied. A few days later I was on my first assignment – covering a non-league football match between Stratford Town and Highgate United. My brief – a mere 400-word match report with teams.

There I was, pristine notebook open at the first page, new pen poised ready to record the cut and thrust of the match.

And I waited...and waited...I put the top back on my pen in case the ink dried up. It was nothing to do with a lack of enthusiasm – more a lack of cut and thrust.

The game ended 0-0 and the only real goal-mouth action came in the last minute of injury time when Highgate hit the Stratford crossbar.

400 words? You're having a laugh, right?

To my astonishment I managed to knock out a half-decent report – to length – and typed it up (these were the days before laptops – at least in my house) and dropped it into the office.

They obviously thought I had done okay as I continued to submit match reports for two seasons, also moving on to the dizzy heights of covering Racing Club Warwick and VS Rugby, teams of a slightly higher standing. Those matches required supplying running copy to the Saturday evening sports paper in Birmingham (teams before kick-off, 50 words after 20 minutes, another 50 at half-time, a further 50 after 60 minutes, then the result and a couple of pars intro on the full-time whistle).

More fun there as these were the days before mobile phones (at least in my house) so filing the copy meant having to leave the action to find a phone – usually in the bar. Just don't ask me about a game at Warwick, where a goal had been scored while I was phoning in copy which I dutifully reported. I found out later that it had been disallowed for offside. Nobody told me. I still burn up at the thought of it even now.

Anyway, on moving back to my native Yorkshire I fell lucky again when the freelance non-league football writer on a well-respected regional daily was just about to leave his post. Armed with my bumper cuttings file (a vital commodity for anybody seriously thinking of entering journalism) I called in and got the job.

That in turn led to my first professional job as a sports reporter on the Scarborough Evening News where I stayed for three years before being head-hunted by the editor of the paper I have now worked on for about 14 years.

Sports journalism is a specialist field, despite what some people may believe. It requires an in-depth and up-to-date knowledge of many sports. Okay, it's good to specialise but you can be more valuable to an overworked sports editor if you can turn your hand to a number of sports.

Passion in your subject(s) is also a must. Journalists need to be able to pass on that knowledge and passion in an entertaining, uncluttered way.

My sports editor tells budding journalists that space in newspapers is premium so stick to the facts – cut out the waffle yet make sure you manage to put the relevant points across. Good advice.

As mentioned earlier, keeping a cuttings file is vital. This serves as your calling card. Most editors worth their salt will want to see examples of your work, neatly presented and covering as many different sports and disciplines (match reports, features etc) as possible. This is to show your versatility. Think quality at all times.

But, how do you go about building up a cuttings file?

Local newspapers are the obvious places to start. A significant part of my job entails subbing submitted match reports from amateur and junior clubs. Somebody has to write those reports and while you will not get paid it could be a good way of building up contacts and that all-important clippings file.

Get in touch with the sports editor. Ask if they would like you to submit a report on a local amateur game. They may say yes and if you deliver good copy to length and on time then the chances are that they will look on you favourably if you offer to do it on a regular basis. Again, don't expect to get paid. Experience is the important thing at this stage. Then, if an opportunity does arise where you could submit on a freelance basis, you are in a much better position to put yourself forward.

It is not just print outlets that could provide an opening. The growth of the Internet means that there are numerous possibilities. It should be easy enough to find blogging sites or online publications. It has to be worth anybody's while approaching the editors/managers of these sites and offering your writing services.

Again, the financial rewards may not be huge. The key on starting out is to become established and see where it takes you from there.

Also, many colleges offer courses on sports journalism and it would be well worth searching on the Internet to find which offers the kind of course you would like to do.

Sports journalism is hard work but very rewarding. I have interviewed numerous top sports stars and still get a tremendous buzz from doing it.

If you have the passion then you are halfway there.

Different Forms of Freelance Writing:
Part VII

Travel Writing

Despite being in the middle of a recession at the time of writing this book, travel writing is still one of the most lucrative and interesting forms of freelance writing available to a freelance writer.

Aside from a few specialist titles, the majority of general magazines and newspapers run a travel section and that's not to mention all the travel companies and inflight publications available. They all need content and if you are interested in travelling, then this could be a viable market for you.

And although it helps if you do travel, you don't necessarily have to go travelling to become a travel writer: there is so much information available nowadays on the Internet that if you have a way with words, you can convince your reader that you have actually visited Australia or Italy or wherever.

Most publications that run a travel page will have a travel editor who will commission pieces and this is the person you should contact. Bear in mind that commissions will be required well in advance of publication, so if you are looking at pitching summer holiday features then you should contact the travel editor at least three months in advance, so that the piece can be planned in to the issue.

If you are a regular traveller, you can easily earn money while you're on holiday. If, for example, you are already going somewhere with your family and you think a publication might be interested in featuring the country you are visiting, get in touch as soon as you have booked your trip and see if they are interested in a feature from you. It doesn't necessarily have to be a trip to somewhere exotic either – many people want to know about travelling to less exotic climes. Readers of the travel pages are just as interested in knowing about things to do with the kids in Scotland as they are in Barbados.

As with any pitch you make to a magazine or newspaper, ensure that you tailor your feature to suit the publication you are pitching to. So if, for example, you are going on a holiday to France, a magazine aimed at mothers with young children would be interested in knowing about what is available there for families. Are there any water parks nearby? What are the facilities for babies and toddlers? What are the local hotels like? If you were targeting a magazine or newspaper aimed at students, then your feature would need to focus on cheap travel and what the nightlife is like there. If you were looking at writing for the more mature generation, they would want to know more about the culture of the country and where they could eat out, or what activities were available to them.

A good travel writer should be able to tailor one destination at various different markets and as a result, gain several different commissions for different publications.

If you enjoy travelling then this is something that you could earn good money out of as a freelance writer.

Different Forms of Freelance Writing: Part VIII

Business Writing

Business writing covers a multitude of things from writing web content for an online company to writing a business brochure and you will be amazed at the amount of businesses out there that know little or nothing about compiling business-related text. They may be brilliant at running their business but when it comes to promoting themselves to their customers, they can often find they hit a road-block. You don't necessarily need web-related experience to be able to offer to write the pages of a website for a business. What you do need is the skills to be able to write concise copy that their customers will understand. If, however, you do have some html experience and knowledge you can offer a complete web design package to small businesses and have your very own lucrative writing business.

If this sort of writing appeals to you then you should start by contacting small and local businesses to see if you can offer them something that will help them generate more money. This could be a new company brochure, a monthly newsletter, business cards, or advertisement wording. You will be surprised at the amount of small businesses that still don't have a website, for example. Offer a small sample of what you can do for them by way of a mock website or a mock brochure.

There are several websites out there that employ freelance business writers on a commission or one-off fee basis, but these can often be hard to break into because a lot of them consist of bidding wars and the freelancer prepared to put in the lowest quote is the one that will win the bid. I always tell writers to value their worth (see Writing is a Proper Job). Writing is hard work and if you constantly accept very little pay for doing what in reality is something that not everyone is capable of doing then you will never be able to make any real money as a freelancer.

Contact your local governmental business centre or your local bank. They might be willing to put you in touch with up and coming businesses that might be looking for someone to help them with their business material.

Many online businesses require someone to maintain their company blogs or Twitter accounts and these are often advertised on freelance writing websites – just remember that updating information on a daily basis will eat into your writing time, so the payment needs to be adequate to make it worth your while.

It's not only businesses that require written content: charities are all in competition with each other to raise much needed funds for their good causes and constantly need to get information across to the general public. Again, most of the big charities will have a budget for this type of work.

Writing Non-fiction Books: Part I

Ideas

We've touched on various opportunities for the freelance writer throughout this book and another very profitable one is writing non-fiction books, so for the next few sections I'm going to concentrate on how you go about getting a non-fiction book published...

Over the past 15 years, I have had 11 non-fiction books published, on a variety of subjects and in that time have learned a lot about how the publishing industry works. It's true that a non-fiction book is easier to get published than a work of fiction, BUT, and this is a big BUT (hence the capitals), as with works of fiction, you still have to convince a publisher that your book is commercially viable. In other words, a lot of people are going to want to buy your book. If you can't prove to the person who is going to invest a minimum of £25,000 in producing, promoting and marketing your book (which is roughly how much it costs to launch a new book), a publisher won't take the gamble.

So, what works and what doesn't? Non-fiction books generally fall into two categories: humour or information. The first category of humour is often one of the hardest genres to write, because one person's humour can differ enormously to another's. Observational humour, such as *The Grumpy Old Women/Men* series, or my very own, *Oh My God, I'm 40!* (a satirical look at women turning 40) often sell well because this type of book is written for a specific audience who can relate to the contents, but you do have to go carefully when coming up with an idea for a humour book: it needs to appeal to a specific audience, but not be so limited that you have no audience.

Learn to Speak Cat by Anthony Smith, for example, is a very funny book about understanding what your cat is saying to you and what every meow means. With over 38% of people in the UK and roughly 86.4 million Americans owning cats as pets, the author already had a ready-made market of readers for this particular title. So if you are thinking of writing a humour title, check out some statistics beforehand to find out if you too will have a ready-made audience for your book. A book about the humour found in potty training a child, for example, could work well (we've all been there, trying to coax a toddler to pee in the potty rather than on the dog, right?). However, if you write a book about the trials of knitting a jumper you probably wouldn't convince a publisher that it will be a best-seller.

The second option for writing a non-fiction book is to write an information book – which is a whole lot easier to write than a humour title, particularly if you know your subject well. Information books again fall into many different categories: self-help, education, computing, cookery, religion, autobiography, misery memoirs, animals, science, health, family, lifestyle, alternative therapies, homes and gardens are just some of the sub-genres that all come under the heading of a non-fiction book. If you are experienced in a subject or are prepared to learn about it, you can write about it. For example, if you have successfully bred a particular breed of dog, or you know how to teach dogs tricks, this is something that you can pass on to others. You might be brilliant with new technology and know how to format electronic books for the Kindle and can write instructions in an easy-to-read style that would benefit other people who want to know how to publish an eBook. Maybe you have worked as an alternative therapist and can pass on your knowledge of working with crystal energy or Reiki.

A novel has to appeal to a much bigger audience than a non-fiction book, so your chances of getting a publishing deal for a non-fiction title are much better than if you were trying to become a novelist. However, as I have said before, publishing is a business and a publisher will only ever take on a book if they are sure they will recoup their investment. If you believe recent industry statistics, 70% of books published do not earn back their advances and 73% of books published do not even make a profit, so you can understand just why publishers are more cautious than ever. A quick look at the UK non-fiction top ten best-sellers list reveals an assortment of interesting titles including auto-biographies from people winning against all odds, football-related books and cookery books, so really anything goes, as long as you can provide something that a fairly widespread audience will be interested in.

Next time you're in a book shop or online, take a look at which non-fiction books are in the charts. Do any of them spark an idea? Think about what you already know or have learned in your life, for instance Maria McCarthy wrote a very successful book called, *The Girls' Guide to Losing Your L-Plates* – a light-hearted and down to earth book about how to pass your driving test with ease. Whilst you may think your life is pretty ordinary, there are many skills that you have already learned that you can pass on to others: learning to drive, getting a job, getting married, bringing up a child, being a step-parent, getting divorced, learning to paint, holidaying alone, learning to dance, going to college, fortune telling – if you can come up with a nice new angle, you are halfway there.

In the next section we will be looking at how to approach a publisher with your idea and why you don't need to write the whole book to get a publishing deal.

Writing Non-fiction Books: Part II

Submitting Your Proposal

So now you have an idea or two about what would work as a non-fiction book, it's time to put those ideas into some sort of proposal for a publisher. Whilst it is correct that it is easier to get a non-fiction publishing deal than a fiction publishing deal and you don't necessarily need an agent to secure one, the publishing side of things for all books is the same – the book will still go through the same publishing process, which means it will generally take between 12 and 18 months before you see your book on the shelves of book stores.

Of all the books I've had published, I've never once needed an agent to help me secure a deal and I have never written the complete book before getting a deal. In fact, publishers of non-fiction often prefer it if you don't write the entire book before submitting it to them, because there will always be things they will want to change, or suggestions they would like to offer, to make the book better or more commercial.

I'll talk more later about the publishing process of a non-fiction book, but for now here is what to do once you have an idea for a non-fiction book...

Write a proposal: A proposal is an outline or synopsis of what your book is going to be about. So, if for example you have an idea for a book about how to live well on a budget (always a good subject in times of recession), you would detail what your book is about, how it differs from other similar books already published, list similar books already available (if there is already a market, this tells a publisher it is a subject that will sell), who your book will appeal to and why you are qualified to write this particular title. This is your chance to sell your idea, so take your time on it. You have to convince a lot of people within the publishing company that it is worth investing in you, so make sure you include as much positive information as possible, including any statistics that will benefit your subject, not forgetting to tell them if your book is to be part of a series.

Write a chapter outline: Your proposal will not secure you a publishing deal on its own. A publisher will want to know what you plan to put into each chapter, how many chapters the book will have – remember, most non-fiction books are a lot shorter than the average word count of a novel, so you will be looking at a total word count of around 30,000–50,000 words for a book. But check the publisher's catalogue to see how long most of their books are, as they will vary. One publishing company I have worked for prefers books of between 30,000 and 35,000 words because they deal with a lot of translation rights and their research has shown that the countries involved like shorter books. When you write your chapter outline, briefly explain in one or two paragraphs what each chapter will be about. As per our example above: chapter one might be an introduction to inform the reader about the book, chapter two might be how to save money on grocery shopping, chapter three might be tips on how to save money on your car and household insurance, and so on.

A few sample chapters: Although you won't need to write the entire book, a publisher will want to see what your writing style is like and how you will go about writing the proposed chapters for your book, so include a few sample chapters. They don't need to be in any particular order, but it is always best to include the introduction or the first chapter. Always make sure your sample chapters are written to industry standards – double-lined spacing, numbered pages, written only on one side of A4 paper and in a recognisable font (usually Times Roman).

A letter of introduction: As with any letter to a commissioning editor, your letter of introduction should be a) professional and b) to the point. Introduce yourself, explaining why you think the publisher would be interested in your book – make sure you have checked their website to ensure they don't already have a similar title to your own and that they are open to submissions.

A CV or Writers' Biography: This will tell a publisher a bit more about you and also why you feel qualified to write a book for them. You don't have to present a whole list of writing experience; in fact you don't necessarily have to have had any prior writing experience. You may have no writing experience but plenty of experience/knowledge of your subject and this is what your CV will tell a publisher. Again, be positive. You don't need to highlight the fact that you may not have written a thing since school. Instead emphasise why you are qualified to write about your chosen subject. You may have been a midwife 'in a previous life' and delivered hundreds of babies, or you may have served in the TA for years, or taught yourself how to earn money from the Internet; you don't necessarily have to have any previous writing experience. Also make sure you include your contact details on your CV.

A stamped addressed envelope: It sounds obvious, but you'd be surprised at how many people either forget to put an SAE in with their proposal, or put the wrong postage on the envelope.

Some publishers, such as Compass Books, part of the John Hunt Publishing company, who have published this book, have come in to the 21st century and are open to email submissions, but not all publishers are as modern!

This is usually all you will need to secure a publishing deal for a non-fiction book. In the next section I will explain what happens next if a publisher is interested, what sort of advances you could be looking at and publishing contracts.

Writing Non-fiction Books: Part III

Advances and Trade Fairs

At this stage in the publishing process you will have sent your proposal to your chosen publisher and if they like the idea, they will contact you by letter or email saying they are interested in your proposal. It's usually at this stage and before signing a contract, that the commissioning editor will want to ask questions, make additional suggestions and will ask how long you think it will take you to write the book, what your estimated word count will be, how you might be able to help with the marketing of this book, etc.

There are many publishing companies nowadays that prior to offering a contract will take a book proposal to trade fairs, such as the London Book Fair, making up a mock copy of the book with samples taken from your proposal and a mock cover. This doesn't mean that it's a guaranteed deal, by any means. Publishing is such a competitive business at the moment and publishers need to be sure that your book is going to generate interest. They might even wait until they have confirmation from their foreign co-publishers that they will buy x amount of books before they offer you a deal.

This recently happened to me: a book I proposed to a publisher went through the process of being designed and packaged for the trade fairs. Unfortunately there just wasn't enough foreign interest for this particular book, so it has been put on hold. Fortunately, the same publisher has asked me to write another book for them.

Publishers have various ways of predicting how much they will make from a particular book and they won't take on a book unless they can be sure that they will make a profit, so when you do get accepted by a publisher, you can be sure that they are not just being nice by taking you on! They have very carefully worked out and calculated exactly how much profit they will make from your writing. Of course not all published books make a profit, and this is the gamble that publishers have to take, which is why you hear 'no thanks' more than 'yes please'. No publisher will ever take a book on if they feel it will make a loss, so when you get that 'yes please', you can be assured that the publisher has thought long and hard about investing their own time and money into publishing your book and really believes that they will recoup that investment and make a profit. Publishing is a business – always remember that.

Another thing that the publisher will take in to account when working out how much profit they are going to make is the writer's advance. Years ago an advance would be paid to an author so that they could afford to work on their next book, until the royalties came in. These days author advances are a lot lower (unless of course you are a high-profile celebrity), and they are paid in three, sometimes four instalments: upon signing your contract, on delivery of your contract, on the publication of your book and sometimes, if it is paid in quarters, upon paperback publication.

The amount of advance you will get for a non-fiction book varies between publisher. Nowadays many don't pay anything and some authors prefer this, because it means that when their book is out in the shops they start earning royalties straight away. If you have an advance, you have to pay back the amount you were paid out of your royalty payments before you earn any further money from that book and research shows that the majority of books do not outsell their advances. As to how much you could expect to get, well, like I say, it all depends on the publisher, and how much money they expect the book will make. You could be offered as little as £400, in which case it won't take you long to start making royalties; or you could be offered several thousand pounds.

There's a huge misconception that once you have a book published you will be financially secure. Research from The Society of Authors showed that 75% of full-time authors earn less than £20,000 per year and the average income for a full-time writer is £16,000 per year, which is why many authors, myself included, need to supplement their income with other freelance writing gigs or take part-time writing work. A very good friend of mine still works full-time as an editor, despite having secured a six-book deal with a publisher. You have to remember also that the publisher is taking all the financial risks with your book, which is why they take 88% of the profits. This is why many authors are also turning to self-publishing their own titles and earning 70% in royalties through publishers such as Amazon Kindle Direct Publishing.

So, it is a huge achievement to have a book accepted by a publisher and if you are prepared to help with the marketing by arranging book signings, talks, etc, you will make a lot more money than if you don't.

Writing Non-fiction Books: Part IV

Contracts

When a publisher offers to publish your book, you will be given a publishing contract or agreement to sign. I would be here all year if I were to go through each and every publisher's contract, but the majority of them are very similar and are known as standard contracts. Although each book contract may vary slightly in its wording, use of rights, etc, they should all include the following information:

Book and Author Information

This is also known as The Works and it is always found on the first page of your agreement. It states who the author is, your address, the title of the book (later referred to as The Works) and the agreement made between the publishing company and yourself.

Rights

The next section is what rights you as the author give to the publisher – often exclusive world rights to print your book. This part will cover all the rights that you are allowing the publisher to use and can include foreign and digital/electronic rights.

Specification and Delivery

This section outlines what the company expects of you as the author and will highlight the dates for delivery of your book. This section will also include agreements to obtain permission, if for example you are using quotes or illustrations in your book. It will also include a note about what will happen if you do not deliver The Works on time, plus notes about proofs and/or any corrections to the proofs, plus any costs that might incur.

Production and Publication

This section in the agreement covers all matters in relation to the production of your book, including: copyright notice, editorial changes, publication date of the book, author copies (you will usually be offered six free copies), revisions, the publisher's requirements and possibly an agreement that you will option your next book to the publisher to consider before offering it to another publisher.

Advance

This section outlines what the publisher is offering you by way of an advance and should stipulate how and when you will be paid. Advances are usually paid in thirds – the first third upon signing the contract, the second upon delivery and the third on the publishing date. However, many publishing companies no longer pay advances to authors.

Royalties

This section will stipulate what percentage of royalties the publisher will pay you (usually between 10 and 12% of NETT sales) and will be broken down in to sub-sections of print rights (hardback and paperback), electronic rights, subsidiary rights and foreign rights.

Accounting

This section will outline how and when you will be paid. Publishers usually pay once or twice a year for the previous six- or 12-month period and should state an accounting date.

VAT

If you are VAT registered then this section will outline any VAT requirements such as your VAT number. Additional accounting information will be included in this section, including foreign payments, withholding taxes and calculation of earnings.

Authors' Warranties and Indemnity

This section stipulates any clauses in the agreement that you are signing for; for example, that The Work is original and has not been published elsewhere. It will also ensure that your work is within the law and sets out liability instructions if the publisher feels that alterations need to be done to The Work prior to publication.

Copyright Infringement

This section ensures that the author will meet any costs that may incur from infringement of copyright.

Termination

This section sets out the situation if the publishers have to terminate the agreement, including how much notice they have to give and under what circumstances should they decide to terminate the agreement.

Death of the Author

This section details what happens if an author dies while the agreement is in force.

Notices

This outlines how any notices relating to the contract between the two parties will be sent, for example by fax, email, post or phone.

Schedule

This part will detail the publishing schedule from acceptance to publication and may or may not include a marketing proposal.

Signatures

There will be a signature from someone (usually the commissioning editor) on behalf of the publishing company and a space for the author to sign. You should be sent two copies; sign both and return one to the publishing company and keep one for your own records.

It is always advisable to read your contract thoroughly and if you don't understand anything, ask for it to be explained to you – legal jargon can be very confusing! It is also advisable to get your contract checked by a solicitor that specialises in contract law or by The Society of Authors. Once you have an acceptance from a publisher, you qualify to join the SOA (for about £90 per year) who will check any contracts and agreements for free and offer you free advice regarding your contract. If you have an agent, he/she will do this for you.

Obviously no two contracts are going to be exactly the same, and publishing companies differ in their specifics, so this is just a guide of what should be in your contract. Once you are happy with your contract and have signed it, the work really begins in the form of marketing your book. We will look at this next.

Writing Non-fiction Books: Part V

Marketing

Once you have signed your contract with a publisher there is often a long delay in the time from signing to seeing your book in print (usually about 18 months), but that doesn't mean it has been forgotten. It takes this long because in the world of publishing, things move at a snail's pace. Having said this, they do move – eventually!

Once a contract has been signed you will be assigned an editor who will work with you from now until your book is in the shops. He/she will contact you with any queries, proofs, suggestions for book cover designs and will want to know any marketing ideas that you might have. This will usually be in the form of a long questionnaire that you will have to fill out detailing anyone and everyone you might know who could help to plug your book.

In the 'good ole days' a writer wrote – end of. There would be a separate publicity department who would do all the ground work to market your book, whilst you got on with writing the next one. Nowadays publishers expect authors to do the majority of marketing for their own books and this includes arranging book signings, press interviews, setting up websites, blogs, etc and anything else you can think of to get your name 'out there'. If you're very lucky you will be assigned a PR person who will help by arranging flyers, bookmarks and other promotional material for your signings, but ultimately it will be up to you to market your own book.

It's important to remember that most commercially printed books from mainstream publishers have a shelf-life of around three months. That's three months in which you have to sell your book. Once the three-month period is up, your book is old news as far as the publishing industry is concerned and will be highly discounted if it is not seen to be attracting big sales. Added to this, the majority of books do not sell out their advances, which is why marketing is so important. Without constant marketing, your book will be dropped from the publisher's lists and the only place customers will find it is in The Works or used copies on Amazon.

The publicity department will want to see where you think you could market your book before it is printed, so if you can convince the local radio station to have an interview with you, or if you belong to a group of people where you can give a talk and do a book signing, then tell them. They might only generate a small number of sales, but this is better than nothing and it keeps your name in the spotlight. If you've written for any newspapers or magazines, ask the editor if they will mention it for you.

Even adverse marketing can be beneficial: recently an author who published her book with Amazon Kindle asked an online book reviewer to review her book. The reviewer didn't like it and said so. The author then decided to challenge him on his review forum, eventually telling him in no uncertain terms where to stick his review. This generated huge sales of her book, if only from readers who wanted to know how dire her book really was!

Whilst I don't suggest this as a marketing tactic, it just goes to prove the adage that there is no such thing as bad publicity – although I don't think many people will take that particular author's work seriously again, given the aggressive attack on this particular reviewer!

When you think about the marketing for your book, write a list of everyone you know and how they might be able to help you: your family, where they work, your own work colleagues, neighbours, schools, clubs and societies. Do you have a background story to your book? All these things can be turned into a marketing opportunity to sell your book.

Most publishers will sell your book to you at a hugely

discounted rate of around 50%, so it is worth ordering some copies for yourself. Whilst you cannot sell them back to trade shops, there is nothing to stop you doing a book signing at a local venue, taking them to your local pub or selling them from the boot of your car, if you so wish.

Next we are going to look at what happens when your book is in the shops, options for future books and the future of the publishing industry, including the revolution of eBooks.

Writing Non-fiction Books: Part VI

The Book Industry

It usually takes between 12 and 18 months from signing a publishing contract to seeing your book stocked in a book store, but with more and more independent book stores going out of business and Waterstones (the UK's largest book retailer) closing many of its stores, publishers and authors are relying heavily on online book shops such as Amazon and Barnes & Noble (America's biggest book retailer and distributor).

Obviously with fewer book shops on the High Street, it means that authors have to adapt to creating a good online presence if they are going to make sales, which means creating a website, a blog, and joining social networks and forums where readers can find them.

Even the book shops that are surviving are limited by shelf space – the majority of new books are given a shelf-life of 12 weeks before they are moved to the 'bargain basement' of the store. Don't be fooled by the huge promotional signs that are displayed in the windows of book shops either – the publisher/ author has to buy this window space. Money talks in the book industry and if you have enough money your book can take pride of place in every window display of every book store in the county. Book shop managers don't choose a book on its reading merit for their window display – it costs and it costs a lot of money.

With the introduction of Amazon's electronic book reader, Kindle, more and more people are buying their books online and downloading them straight to their computers, iPads, iPhones or electronic readers. It has been said that eReaders are to books what iTunes is to music and many experts within the publishing industry are predicting that eBooks are the way forward. The majority of mainstream publishers are turning their backlist of titles into eBooks and new books will now automatically be published in hardback, paperback and eBook formats. All this is making authors rethink the whole publishing process. With Amazon introducing Kindle Direct Publishing, it means that authors can write and edit their books, upload them on the KDP website and be selling them to millions of people worldwide, within minutes. No longer are they tied to trying to find an agent, who then has to find a publisher, and then wait a year and half to see their book stocked in a book store. They are cutting out the middle-men and doing it for themselves – and with better royalty payments.

Traditional publishers pay between 10 and 12% in royalties and that's not taking in to account the 12–15% you will also pay to your agent, if you have one. Amazon pay between 35 and 70% royalties and there have been some very successful stories from authors who have opted to work with Amazon, rather than take the traditional route. They will also provide a hard-copy (paperback) version of your book if you don't just want to have your work formatted as an eBook.

Even though I have had 10 books published the traditional way, I decided as an experiment to try Kindle Direct Publishing for a novel, *Oh Great, Now I Can Hear Dead People*, that I had written a few years ago. Although I did secure an agent for this particular book, she didn't manage to find a home for it and it was just languishing in my PC gathering metaphorical dust, so I decided to put it onto Amazon Kindle. That novel has been in the top ten best-seller charts for women's fiction and supernatural fiction ever since and I have made more money in royalties on this one title in the space of a month than many of my traditionally published titles. The novel has now been taken on by my publisher, John Hunt Publishing, under their Soul Rocks imprint to be reproduced as a paperback.

Best-selling thriller writer, Stephen Leather, who has

published with Harper Collins, also decided to take some of his books that his publishers had turned down and try them on Amazon Kindle. Leather makes thousands of pounds in sales each month as do many other authors. So it really is worth thinking about, because most people in the publishing industry agree that eBooks are the way forward, which is brilliant news, especially for first-time authors who want to test the market with their work, or have a niche product they want to market.

If you do decide to go the traditional route, part of your contract will almost certainly include electronic rights, which include eBooks. Part of your contract may also state that your current publisher has the rights of option on your next book/s. This means that you are obliged to give your publisher first refusal on your next book. Whilst this is a good thing, it doesn't necessarily mean they will take it.

After having five books published with London publisher Hamlyn, when I offered them my sixth in the series, they told me that the market had become too saturated and that they were no longer publishing in that genre, but my contract stipulated that I had to offer future books to them first before I offered them to another publisher.

The publishing industry is changing fast and you really do need to keep up with everything that is going on, by looking at websites such as The Bookseller or other publishing industry websites.

Motivation, Self-belief and Doubts

There's a wise saying that goes: if you always do what you've always done, you'll always get what you always got. Or in other words, if you don't take chances or change the way you do things, or if you make decisions you're not 100% totally sure of, you will always be where you are now. And this can apply to anything in life: if you keep doing the same thing day in day out, or you fear making a decision, how can you ever move on from where you are now?

Writing is a difficult occupation and if you are hoping to write as a means to earn an income, then your writing relies heavily on an audience willing to pay to read it, whether that be in book form, an article, the lyrics of a song, a screenplay, or whatever. Writing is also very much a solitary occupation and in turn relies on you having a great deal of self-belief and motivation; it doesn't take much to knock you off track. This of course can take the form of a rejection letter from an agent, a publisher or an editor, but is often much closer to home. So many people have told me that someone close to them has shot them down in flames when they have told them of their ideas, often to the extent that they have decided not even to take the chance.

I've experienced this a few times in my career, and very recently too: a distant relative of mine got wind of a new project I had been working on. This relative said that the idea I had was ridiculous, would never work and did I not realise that there was a recession on at the moment?

Being a professional writer, rejections from publishers and editors is part and parcel of the job and in time you learn to accept that it is nothing personal. It's a business, that's all. However, when someone you know and trust tells you that your ideas are rubbish, I challenge anyone to not suddenly have doubts about it. And this is when it becomes a problem.

That idea you had, whether it's a book, a short story, or an article, suddenly seems like not such a good idea after all and those initial dreams you had can be destroyed in one fell swoop. Despite the fact that this particular person has no idea whatsoever about the publishing industry, and I know the industry inside out, it still made me doubt my abilities and my decision.

So what did I do? I sulked for a week, I found support in a couple of close friends and decided that I should go with my initial instinct and just get on with it.

I realised that if I had listened to other people instead of just going with my first thoughts during my career as a writer, I would never have had anything published, and this is what happens to a lot of people: they have an idea, they get excited about its potential then someone comes along and, for want of a better expression, piddles on their bonfire. Invariably this is the moment they lose self-belief, start doubting their abilities and drop the idea altogether, and carry on doing what they've always done. The years pass and they look back and realise that the only thing they have achieved in life is to get older. They haven't moved forward in any way.

I always maintain that nothing you do is ever wasted. You might not get a commission or a book deal for something you've written, but you haven't wasted your time. On the contrary, you've done something with your time; you've created ideas that in time might just be the exact thing that someone else wants to commission from you.

Writers in particular require a lot of self-belief and motivation because more often than not you are working alone and can be your own worst critic; this is amplified when someone else tells you that your idea will never work. So what's the alternative then? You doubt yourself, listen to your objector, don't follow your idea through and continue to live your life never taking a gamble?

Don't let this happen to you. It is nothing more than a waste of time. And if you do have doubts, think: what's the worst thing that can happen? So you spend a year working on your novel and discover that every publisher in the land has rejected it. So? You've written it, haven't you? And how do you know that the next publisher you approach won't love the idea? If you listen to those that tell you it will never work, you will never do it and you will never know what might have been. How do you know that the children's book you wrote won't be the exact thing a publisher is looking for? Who'd have thought that stories about vampires would be a phenomenal success? I bet you Stephenie Meyer didn't take any notice of those who told her that her idea to write a book based on vampires would never work.

If you find you are lacking self-belief and are full of doubts – particularly when someone else doubts your abilities – think about the quote at the beginning of this chapter. Are you going to not take a chance purely on the basis that someone else thinks it's not a good idea? If you don't even try, you will never know whether it will be a success or not. Are you going to just continue to do what you've always done?

And this doesn't just apply to your writing. It applies to life in general too. None of us know exactly how long we will be here for. Take chances, take a gamble. Don't doubt yourself just because someone else prefers to play it safe in life. Go with your first instincts and if you do feel doubts creeping in, look for motivational and inspiring stories from people who have taken chances, such as Thomas Edison who said, 'I have not failed, I've found 10,000 ways that won't work.'

Don't end up thinking, 'I wish I'd just done it,' and get left behind.

Seeing Is Believing

The above chapter (originally a post) on motivation and self-belief received more comments than anything else I've put up on my blog, which suggests to me that it is one of those things that bother writers – a lot. So this next chapter is all about visualis-ation tools for a writer and about how to create a vision board to get what you want out of life in terms of being a writer.

Vision boards are a wonderful visual tool to create things that you want in your life and are often mentioned in self-help books/workshops/magazines, etc.

Studies have shown that visual images have a greater effect on us than any other form of communication – this is why adver-tisers have huge advertising budgets worth thousands for TV adverts. When we see an image over and over again, that image sinks in to our subconscious and we can literally picture it in our minds. If we can do this, there is a greater chance of us attaining that image in real life.

Most self-help teachers use vision boards as a means to help us attract the things we all want in life, be it a new home, a car, a good relationship, our chosen career, etc, but this method can also be used to the writer's advantage: you can create a vision board to help you achieve paying commissions, book accep-tances, or even to help you with the progress of your latest novel.

The idea is pretty simple: you find images that represent what it is you want out of your writing career and paste them on to a large sheet of card (or in a notebook if you prefer the world not to know your dreams and desires), you then look at the images on a daily basis. Over a short course of time these images will sink in to your subconscious and because your subconscious can't distinguish between real and imaginary (a good example of this is when we dream), it assumes this is what your life is and in turn, you subconsciously attract opportunities to you, which in turn become reality.

So, for example, if you want to earn higher-paying commissions from your writing, you would find an image to represent this. This could be a picture of a pile of money (Google Images is excellent for this purpose), or a photo of several different magazines and a copy of your letter-headed invoice.

If you harbour dreams of giving up the day job and having your novel in the best-seller charts, you would find images that reflect this; so perhaps a picture of a book-signing with you Photo-shopped into the picture, or make a mock-up of *The Times* best-seller charts with your name and book title listed at number one. Another idea is to write a short sentence to accompany each image, such as, 'editors contact me for commissions' or 'I have secured an agent who has found me a great publisher for my novel.'

Even if you are new to the game, you can still use the vision board technique to help you attain certain writing-related goals. For example, you might have an idea for a new novel, a screenplay, a non-fiction book or a feature. If this is the case, find something that represents your wish, for example, a mock-up of the first page of your manuscript with the sentence, 'the first chapter of my book is written,' or 'the first five minutes of my screenplay is written'.

Seeing these images on a daily basis will not only make you feel better, but will also encourage you to take action, and you will get a tremendous buzz when you can tick off each goal once you've achieved it. Some will take longer than others and I suggest you mix up short and long-term goals in your images. The short-term ones will only take a matter of days or weeks to complete, but by ticking those ones off your vision board it will make it an easier process to get to the bigger ones.

Try it, it really does work!

Writing IS a Proper Job

It always amazes me how many people consider writing to be inferior to other jobs. Whilst I have mentioned earlier in this book the advantages of *occasionally* writing free (*gratis*) to get your foot in the door, this does not mean that people can take advantage of you and expect you to write things for them for nothing. Neither does it mean that people can assume they can interrupt you whenever they feel like it or not take your work seriously.

Unfortunately when you tell someone that you are a writer, you will invariably be quizzed as to what you have had published. If you haven't had anything published the other person automatically assumes that this is some kind of hobby or flight of fancy. Writing in itself is hard work and it takes a lot of self-belief to put down your thoughts in to coherent words that other people will enjoy reading, let alone to have to justify yourself every time someone asks what you do for a living.

Very often it is friends and family that are limited in their support when you tell them that you are a writer – and that is exactly what you are. It doesn't matter whether you have a hundred and one articles published or nothing published yet, as soon as you make that statement that you want to become a writer and you start getting words down on paper, then you are a writer. The moment that you put words onto the screen with the intention of earning money from your writing, is the moment that you are a writer.

So many times I have heard stories of talented people that have had their dreams of being a writer shattered simply because their friends or family have laughed at the very idea of them becoming a writer. Or they have moaned about the time they spend on their computer, demanding their attention instead. Or they negatively criticise what the writer has written.

You have as much chance of becoming a successful writer as

anyone else. Even JK Rowling had her fair share of rejections and remember, rejection is a part of the job of a writer. There is nothing to say that those words you have typed on the screen or scribbled in your notebook on the train to work won't become the next best-seller. Even the publishers don't know what the next big thing will be. Below is a short list of things to do and say whenever you come up against someone who does not take your work seriously:

If someone laughs or mocks you when you tell them you are a writer:

It can be hard when you first broach the subject that you are going to be a writer to friends and family and if they make negative or disparaging remarks it can knock your confidence for six. If someone takes the Mickey out of you, or tells you that you'll never be a writer, take a deep breath and recite those famous words that Thumper from the *Bambi* film said, 'If you can't say something nice, don't say nothin' at all.' And walk away with the thought: 'I'll show you.' Whilst it's lovely to have the support of your friends and family, particularly when you want to celebrate getting a commission or commiserate when you get a rejection, if all they are going to do is ridicule you, then you are better off walking away from them with a knowing smile. Have faith in yourself and your abilities and if other people don't want to support you then that is their problem. They will be changing their tune when you start getting paid for your writing.

If someone asks you what you've had published – and you haven't yet:

This is usually the first question you will get asked when you mention that you are a writer and if you have yet to have anything published, and it can be one of those moments when you want the ground to swallow you up. You could try the 'Look! There's a bear!' routine and head for the hills, or you could say, 'I've got a magazine editor considering my work.' Or, 'A publisher might be interested in my novel.' Neither are lies: if you are submitting your work to editors then yes, they will be considering your work and if you are submitting your novel to a publisher, they could well be interested in publishing it, so you are not lying.

If someone asks you what you're writing at the moment:

How you should answer this will depend on whether they are really interested or just being nosey. If they are really interested tell them what it is you are working on at the moment. If they are just being nosey (and a good clue is when they start asking how much money you make as a writer) you have my permission to extend the truth a little: tell them you earn enough, thank you very much, and that you're in talks with Steven Spielberg abut film rights as you speak!

If someone resents you spending time writing:

This is often a writer's spouse, partner, children, other family members or friends. The truth of the matter is that writing takes up time and if someone else feels they deserve to have that time spent on them then resentment can set in. In an ideal and fair world everyone would be entitled to do the things they love when they want to without having demands made of them. Unfortunately it's not always a fair and ideal world. When someone makes you feel guilty that you are spending time on your writing instead of giving them the attention they feel they deserve, calmly explain that this is your time and that after you've finished what you're working on you will pay them attention. It can be difficult running a household, looking after children, holding down a paying job and trying to become a writer all at the same time, without the additional guilt that people will pile on you. Agree between yourself and your family to set yourself a certain time every day that is your writing time, where you will not be disturbed. This could be one hour every evening when the children have gone to bed, or if you're an early bird, first thing in the morning when no one else is awake. You could agree that you have one full, uninterrupted afternoon per weekend or a whole day in the week when the children are at school, or someone can look after them. The main thing is that you get your time to write without feeling guilty for doing so. Again, if you present to people that it is 'just a hobby' or just something that you dabble in, this is what other people will think; they will think it's unimportant. If you learn to say, 'I have a magazine editor interested in seeing my work,' it puts a whole different light on the matter.

If someone asks you to write their Best Man Speech:

As soon as you start getting paid to write people will assume that you know what you are doing and will respect you for it, which is all very nice, but they often then assume that you are on hand to write their Best Man speech, romantic poem to go in a card, write an essay entitled, *How the Government has Let Us Down – discuss*, and edit their novel all in a weekend. Whilst it's very flattering to be asked these things they will eat into your own writing time and you will find that you spend more time reading through or writing someone else's work than getting on with your own projects. I once had an elderly neighbour who would think nothing of popping round with a pile of notes she had written to the local council complaining about the infrequency of rubbish collections or something or other and expect me to type them all up for her. I would always oblige because I felt sorry for her. Every week she would have a complaint letter for me to write and it was not only my time she was using; it was my electricity, paper, printer ink, envelopes and stamps! It only stopped because I moved house and didn't leave a forwarding address. Just say, 'I'm sorry, I'd love to, but I have an urgent deadline to meet.'

They wouldn't expect a solicitor or another professional to work for nothing, so they shouldn't expect you to do the same.

If someone asks you to put in a good word to your editor/publisher about them:

There will come a time (trust me on this) when you will get paid for your writing, whether it be from writing for magazines and newspapers or writing a screenplay or a novel, or writing a business brochure, an advertising campaign or the web content for someone's website. You will start to become known to editors and/or publishers as a reliable and professional freelance writer and in turn will soon have a list of contacts of people that will buy your work from you. You will also (trust me on this) have your fair share of people (funny enough they are often the ones that showed lack of support when you started out) who will see that you are earning money from your writing and think that they can do the same, but the easy way. They assume they can ask you to put in a good word for them to your editors or publisher and bingo! They too can be a writer. Whilst it is a compliment to be admired and recognised for your hard work (and earning a living from writing is hard work) it is one thing to be complimented and quite another when people think they can use you for a leg up for their own means.

I cannot tell you the amount of times I have received emails asking if I could send stuff on to my editors or publishers, or had requests for the name of a commissioning editor, all because the other person wanted an easy way into the industry. I'm more than happy to help anyone in their quest to be a writer, but when people befriend you simply because they want you to put them in touch with your agent or an editor because they think they will get a commission or a book deal on that basis alone, I'm tempted to say, 'Do you know how many years I have put in to this career?' I don't of course, I'm far too polite; but I have learned to spot the signs when someone is only contacting me because they want a favour and then they are gone again. This is certain to happen to you too. My way of dealing with this is to recommend they buy a copy of *The Writers' and Artists' Yearbook* because all the contact names are in there.

If someone negatively criticises your work:

And they will – it comes with the job; you can't expect everyone to agree with or even like what you have written all of the time. This happens all the time to writers, particularly on online review boards or forums; the best thing to do is to shrug and just accept that it's not their cup of tea. I always advise writers starting out not to share their writing with members of their family or their friends – either they will tell you it's wonderful, regardless of whether it is or not, so as not to upset you, or they will feel qualified to rip it apart (figuratively, not literally), which will upset you. Leave the critiquing of your work to the professionals. If an editor tells you that you've used too many adjectives or that you have no 'hook', they are the ones to listen to. You can go back over your work and rewrite it. Friends and family are usually not qualified to point out your written mistakes.

The same applies to online reviews/critiques. I am not a fan of these websites or forums where you place your work online for the whole world to see and critique and I would never advise a writer to put their work on one of these sites. The reason being is that there are a lot of people out there who have nothing better to do than negatively criticise someone else's work, and what is more take great pleasure in being nasty to others, which can be soul-destroying to the writer. Most of these people are not professional editors and are not qualified to say whether or not a piece of work is 'good' or 'bad', or should have a 'two-star' rating or a 'five-star' rating. If you really want your work critiqued then pay to have it done professionally by people already in the business.

Another interesting thing associated with reviews in particular is that it is often other writers that write in the same genre as the author who are the ones that give scathing reviews. This is something that has happened to me and to other professional writers that I know. Genuine readers will give genuine and usually positive reviews – genuine readers who don't like a book or an article rarely comment on it at all. They have better things to do with their time. Other writers read their competitors' work from a totally different point of view, from a more 'industry' viewpoint and will pick out things such as 'character flaws', 'misuse of dialogue' and 'obvious fillers'.

Again this is part and parcel of the job and the best thing you can do is to let it come and go and don't even pay any attention to it. The worst thing you can do is bite back with a comment. Words are powerful, but often it is silence that is more so.

We have come to the end of this book now and I hope that I have given you plenty of ideas to help you on your journey as a freelance writer. The great thing about being a freelance writer is that you can work anywhere in the world and there are no age-restrictions, so it really can be a career for life and you never know who you might meet on that journey.

Until next time,

Happy writing!

Whilst Deborah won't send you details of her editorial or publishing contacts, she is only too pleased to answer any questions relating to freelance writing. You can find out more at her website

www.deborahdurbin.com

or email

Deborah.durbin@yahoo.com

For book excerpts, publishing rights, etc, please contact Deborah's publisher at:

www.johnhuntpublishing.com

**COMPASS
BOOKS**

Compass Books focuses on practical and informative 'how-to' books for writers. Written by experienced authors who also have extensive experience of tutoring at the most popular creative writing workshops, the books offer an insight into the more specialised niches of the publishing game.